COLLECTING
ANTIQUE
FIREARMS

To Frances

COLLECTING ANTIQUE FIREARMS

DR MARTIN KELVIN

F.S.A. (Scot)

Stanley Paul

London Melbourne Auckland Johannesburg

Stanley Paul & Co. Ltd
An imprint of Century Hutchinson Ltd
Brookmount House, 62–65 Chandos Place,
Covent Garden, London WC2N 4NW

Century Hutchinson Australia (Pty) Ltd
16–22 Church Street, Hawthorn, Melbourne, Victoria 3122

Century Hutchinson New Zealand Limited
PO Box 40–086, Glenfield, Auckland 10

Century Hutchinson South Africa (Pty) Ltd
PO Box 337, Bergvlei 2012, South Africa

First published 1987

Set in 10/11pt Ehrhardt Roman

Printed by Scotprint Ltd, Scotland and bound
by Butler & Tanner Ltd, Frome, Somerset

British Library Cataloguing in Publication Data
Kelvin, Martin
    Collecting antique firearms.
    1. Firearms — Collectors and collecting
    I. Title
    683.4'0075   NK6904

ISBN 0 09 166310 5

Contents

Acknowledgements

I wish to acknowledge the following institutions and individuals for permission to reproduce material in their possession.

To the Library of Congress, Washington D.C., for allowing me to reproduce the fascinating early photograph of Jesse James.

To the Bettmann Archive/BBC Hulton Picture Library, for allowing me to reproduce their interesting photograph of Samuel Colt.

To the Smithsonian Institution, Washington D.C., for permission to reproduce the famous de Gheyn engraving of an arquebusier.

To the Governing Body of Christ Church, Oxford, for permitting me to reproduce the earliest picture of a gun from the de Milemete manuscript.

To the Board of Trustees of the Armouries, H. M. Tower of London, for permission to reproduce a photograph of Alexander John Forsyth.

I would like also to express my grateful thanks to my old friend George Wentworth, who willingly allowed me to handle and photograph his magnificent wheel-lock pistol.

My thanks are also due to Gordon Forrest, who created the exploded diagrams of the various lock mechanisms, and kindly allowed me to reproduce them here.

To my dear friend Fred Tomlinson I am especially indebted, not only for reading the original manuscript, but for his helpful advice and suggestions, especially in relation to the chapter on restoration.

Lastly, I willingly acknowledge the part played by my wife Frances, without whose constant support and encouragement this book would never have been completed.

Foreword

In July 1985, as I sat alone in the lounge of my Galloway retreat reading the inevitable gunbook, the thought occurred to me, which I was unable to suppress, that I should produce a detailed descriptive catalogue of my own collection of antique firearms.

As this idea developed in my mind, it seemed to me that it might be more interesting if I were to expand that theme to encompass all the weapons that had passed through my hands in the seventeen or so years since I began collecting.

In addition, as many of the antique weapons in my collection had undergone a greater or lesser degree of restoration at my own hands, it seemed appropriate to include in my account an accurate description of the extent of such repairs to each pistol.

Accordingly, I set about my task with a will, but it was not long before another complication became apparent.

As I began to handle each individual item, a whole flood of recollections crowded into my mind: where I'd purchased it, the circumstances involved in the sale, the old character who had unearthed the gun in the first place, and a host of other memories.

I decided at that point that my account must be more than simply a catalogue of guns. It must tell the whole story, starting at the very beginning, when the first seeds of the collecting urge were being sown in my mind, and continuing to the present day, embracing the entire spectrum of the strange but fascinating world of the antique gun collector, and at the same time giving the reader some degree of insight into the situations experienced, and the problems encountered, by a devoted *aficionado* intent upon the acquisition of antique firearms.

In order that the reader may become immersed in the lore of his chosen hobby, I have included in my account a short history of the development of the gun, from the discovery of gunpowder to the invention of the metallic cartridge. I have also attempted to give some guidance in the dating of antique firearms, since this information is largely ignored in the standard works, yet is of considerable interest and importance to the collector.

Last of all, I have endeavoured to describe in some detail, and in an entirely practical manner, the little known art of antique firearms restoration, which will, I hope, offer new horizons to the reader, whether he be a collector of some experience or merely standing at the threshold of a fascinating new world.

It should be stated that the weapons illustrated and described in this book are, without exception, in perfect mechanical order, most being in excellent condition. They do not purport to be museum pieces, and represent precisely the sort of weapons that the average collector of antique firearms can confidently expect to acquire.

Origins

'How did you ever start collecting all these things?' people sometimes say to me, regarding me tolerantly as if I were some sort of spoiled child delinquent who requires careful humouring.

Occasionally, if my questioner feels that he or she knows me particularly well, there will be some reference to asserting one's masculinity, and perhaps even of phallic symbolism.

But how did it all really begin? How indeed?

Can there be a man alive whose pulse does not quicken as he raises a flintlock to his eye to take aim?

Does the sharp snap of a closing frizzen and the harsh click of a weapon brought to full cock not ring in his ears like a thunderclap, or the roar of waves crashing against the rocks on the seashore?

Can he not imagine the same sound ringing out in the gathering dusk as the highwayman steps out before the slowing coach, the driver and guard open-mouthed as he harshly cries, 'Stand, and deliver!'?

Is there any person who can hold a duelling pistol in his hand without being transported in a flash to that quiet common on the edge of town, just as the dawn is about to break?

Can he not see the cold mist rising from the ground, the grim faces of the combatants, feel his heart thudding against his breast, as he hears the words: 'Ready, aim, . . . FIRE!'?

What man amongst you has not, in his fantasies, swung from the rigging of a pirate ship, clutching an enormous pistol in one hand and a cutlass in the other, before crashing on to the deck of a hapless merchantman to wreak a dreadful fate on the unfortunate occupants?

I passed my childhood in the years immediately before, and during, World War II, and in common with other children of that period experienced a certain deprivation in practical terms. We did not have toys, other than 'hand-me-downs', and consequently had to make greater use of that much neglected attribute – imagination. The one toy that I wanted more than any other was a simple cap gun, but such luxuries were absolutely unobtainable. Consequently, sticks and stones became magically transformed into Winchester rifles and Colt Peacemakers.

I was taken to my first Western, *The Santa Fe Trail*, and its star, the swashbuckling Errol Flynn, was to become my great hero. Thus began a love affair with the Western that has endured for almost half a century.

Other adventure films soon followed – *Captain Blood, San Antonio, The Sea Hawk*. Could anyone see them and remain unmoved?

Then, in 1966, I was in Wilmslow and noticed a book in a closing-down sale at a newsagents. It was £1 10*s*. and was entitled *The Book of the Gun* by H. L. Peterson, the well-known American collector/writer. Somewhat sheepishly I made the purchase. This book is a fascinating account of the development of the gun, and is undoubtedly one of the best books on arms and armour ever written.

Not long after this I was on holiday in Majorca. In the resort of Porto Cristo, in a souvenir shop, I saw what I believed to be an ancient flintlock pistol. The shop assistant brought it down for me, announcing, 'It was made in Segovia in the same factory as the originals!'

I was astonished, because it looked to me exactly like an old gun. I was determined to purchase it, and duly brought it home to hang on the wall of our lounge.

All my male dinner-guests were attracted by this gun, and they would handle it, cock it, and bring it up to the aim. Everyone accepted it for what it appeared to be – an old flintlock, and I never disillusioned them by telling them the truth.

Yet always I wondered, 'How can one tell the difference between the reproduction and the genuine article?', and this question fascinated me for a long time.

Even now, people say to me, 'How can you tell the difference?' The answer, of course, is in a single word – experience. And experience only comes from handling scores and scores of such weapons over a period of many years. And despite even this, experienced collectors do make mistakes, and can be caught out by carefully distressed reproductions.

About this time, an advertisement appeared in the *Sunday Express* – 'Antique revolvers for sale – look like Colts, only an expert can tell the difference. £5, £10, or £15, depending on condition.'

I sent in my £15 and waited eagerly for the post. What a disappointment awaited me! When the gun arrived, it was certainly ancient, that was indisputable. It was also very rusty, and it did not work. The gun was what a collector would recognize today as one of the cheap continental copies of Colt's Patent revolvers. Even when new it could not compare with the Colt. I wasn't an expert, yet, but I *could* tell the difference. And so I returned the gun and asked for a refund of my money.

But the seeds had been firmly sown, and I was

shortly to make a purchase that would change my life.

I had found a small antique shop in Stockport and had observed it for some time, and it always seemed to have interesting articles inside.

One day I took the fatal step and crossed the threshold into a whole new world. The proprietor, Fred Tomlinson, was to become one of my closest friends. In a cabinet he had several antique pistols and one in particular took my fancy. It was a percussion belt pistol by Henneker of Chatham, and appeared to be in excellent condition. I was a little perturbed by the pitting on the barrel, and the broken nipple, but the proprietor seemed confident that he could repair these, and mentioned something about rebrowning the barrel and turning a new nipple, neither of which I understood. After a few days I returned to the shop and proudly bore away my new purchase.

I was really thrilled by this gun, although there was little I could do to it, in view of its excellent condition, other than strip it down in order to study the lock mechanism. However, I was able to clean and polish the trigger-guard, which was ingrained with dirt and rust, and clean the interior of the barrel, which was similarly affected.

I was very fortunate to meet Fred Tomlinson who taught me all I know about such antique firearms. He had started collecting and repairing antique guns when only a boy. He trained as an engineer, and had, when I met him, not long opened up as a general antiques dealer.

Fred knows more about antique guns than anyone I have ever met, and his engineering skills, of course, made him an ideal person to carry out any repair work. He was also quite willing and ready to tell me all I wanted to know.

Gradually, picking up a bit of knowledge here and a bit there, I amassed sufficient information to allow me into the magic world of antique firearms restoration, but perhaps the greatest acclamation, the Gold Seal of approval, as it were, is when Fred passes on a gun to me to repair and polish the stock.

How often, in the past, have I gone round to his shop, proudly bearing the latest acquisition, which I deliver into his hands, and await the expected murmurs of approval, only to see him studying the weapon for what seems an eternity, turning it over and over thoughtfully, as his frown gets deeper and still deeper.

Finally, he would say something like, 'It's a pity the barrel's been shortened,' or, 'Did you see where the trigger-guard's been welded?' or 'Was it you who fitted the replacement hammer?' And, of course, I would go away thinking, 'That's the last antique gun I'll ever buy.'

But this is how knowledge is built up, the only way that one can become experienced, and it is certainly a long, hard road.

It was Fred who sold me my first lathe, and gradually I acquired some proficiency in making a few of the parts so essential to the restorer, screws of all kinds, of which I must have made hundreds, slotting the screw heads with a hacksaw, and filing in the taper always found in antique gunscrews.

Ramrods, ramrod tips, ramrod pipes, worms and jags, ebony-handled turnscrews and nipple keys, ivory studs for gunboxes, top-jaw screws, tumbler screws and sidenails – it was a marvellous time. And what a sense of achievement when a job had been satisfactorily completed!

Of course, in those days, there were lots of old guns about. It was not uncommon to find weapons in ordinary antique shops. They were always turning up and, if in poor condition, could be readily obtained without first having to consult your bank manager. Unfortunately, the situation has changed for the collector. The best guns are locked away, either in bank vaults as investment items or in the hands of collectors, who do not want to sell what they have, although they are unable to add to their collections.

Prices have shot up, and the guns available tend to be in the hands of the specialist gun dealers, of whom there are now very many.

Life for the collector of antique firearms is not, I am afraid, what it was.

But to get back to the early days, this was how it all began . . . .

Robert Wogdon

WOGDON, Robert (1760–1797)
Shops in London and Ireland. Made
flintlock pocket pistols. Also coach
pistols and fowling-pieces. Made cased
duelling pistols of fine workmanship.

Not long after meeting Fred Tomlinson, I walked into an antique shop in Paisley in Scotland that had not been opened long, and lying there was a rusted and pitted old flintlock, minus its cock, with great chunks of woodwork missing, the rest riddled with woodworm, and a broken frizzen spring.

I happily walked out of the shop with my new acquisition, which cost me the princely sum of £6. I could see by the way my in-laws were looking at me that they were entirely convinced that I was insane.

Little did I know, at that time, that I was clutching in my hot little hand a product of one of the most famous pistol makers in the England of the 1780s – a Wogdon duelling pistol.

In the courts of the time, if a matter could not be settled by due process of law, it was referred to as a Wogdon case, meaning, that only a duel could settle the outcome. Robert Wogdon even had the dubious distinction of having a poem written about him, which began,

'Hail, Wogdon,
Patron of that leaden death.'

I delivered the gun into the hands of my new-found friend and asked if he could repair it for me. However, he seemed more anxious to purchase the weapon than to repair it. I explained that I thought the gun was a duelling pistol – the signature on the pitted lockplate and the barrel were both very indistinct – and that I was keen to restore the piece rather than sell it. Fred promised to replace the cock, top-jaw and screw, and the frizzen spring, but insisted that I repair the stock myself. But how? Fred explained the main principles of stock repair, gave me two pieces of walnut, and off I went to read Lister's book, *Antique Guns – Their Care, Repair, and Restoration.*

Finally I was ready, and, preparing my own wood filler, carefully filled each wormhole. I spliced in the new wood, and, when the glue had set, shaped it to allow the barrel to rest once more within the stock. Then I sanded the whole stock, rendering the surface smooth by applying successive grades of fine sandpaper.

I was delighted with the result, and took the gun back to Fred. To my surprise, he was somewhat critical of my efforts and patiently explained that, with a gun of this quality, the stock and barrel should be a tight fit, and showed me how this could be achieved. I went off once more, did the job as instructed, and again returned. This time I received the seal of approval.

My next task was to file the octagonal barrel to remove all traces of pitting, and subject the lockplate to the same treatment, finally working through successive grades of wet and dry sandpaper until the metal surfaces were smooth and highly polished.

In the meantime, Fred had constructed a new cock, top-jaw and screw, as well as a new frizzen spring. I had no idea at that time what all this entailed.

First, one has to study photographs, not just of duelling pistols, but of Wogdons, in order to determine the correct shape of the new cock. Then this must be hand filed from a piece of carbon steel. The cock must be drilled and filed off square to accept the tumbler, and a tumbler screw made and slotted. Finally a top-jaw must be constructed, and a top-jaw screw turned in the lathe and the thread cut with dies. Making a spring is a very tedious business, and is followed by tempering. Sometimes, if the latter process is

Flintlock duelling pistol by Robert Wogdon

not quite correct, the spring will break on taking any pressure, and the whole process must be started all over again. The restoration was completed by engraving the swan-neck cock with single-line engraving, re-engraving the newly 'struck-up' lockplate and barrel with the maker's name, Wogdon, in script and, finally, rebrowning the barrel and constructing an appropriately tipped ramrod.

When completed, none of these repairs was obvious, except under very close scrutiny. The entire restoration took literally hundreds of hours, but taught me so much about the restoration of antique guns that its worth to me could not be measured.

After some years I sold the gun in a deal, for twenty times the figure that I had originally paid.

Flintlock Pocket Pistol by Twigg

TWIGG, T. (1760–1780)
Famous London gunsmith. Made
multishot flintlock pistols and 4-barrelled
ducksfoot pistol. Name changed to
Twigg & Bass, 1780–1783. Made cased
duelling pistols and holster pistols. Name
reverted to Twigg, 1783–1813. Made
flintlock pocket pistols and holster
pistols.

Length: 6½ in.
Barrel length: 1½ in.
Bore: 0.48 in.

Such pistols were often made in the provinces, such as Birmingham, and stamped with Birmingham proof marks. They were then delivered to London gunsmiths like Twigg, and were engraved with his name, which would obviously make the gun easier to sell.

This particular pistol is well made, and is beautifully engraved on either side of the frame with trophies of arms. The weapon has much of its original finish, browning being still in evidence around the frame and trigger-guard. This type of gun is known as a boxlock with centre-swung hammer, the cock being the 'throat-hole' variety. The butt is of rosewood, and is slabsided. The barrel is of the 'turn-off' variety, being unscrewed by means of a barrel key for loading, using a slightly oversized ball, so rendering the use of wadding unnecessary. Engraving on this pistol consists of the maker's name engraved in Roman lettering on the left side of the frame, while the right side is engraved 'London'. A sunburst is engraved on the trigger-guard, while the sliding safety is engraved in herring-bone pattern. Proof marks are post-1813 Birmingham type. The sliding safety, which lies on the top strap, locks the cock at half-bent.

It is said that genuine Twigg pistols were always engraved in script, not Roman lettering, as on this example, but I dispute this statement, since although such pistols are of Birmingham manufacture, Twigg himself obviously considered that they were of sufficiently high quality to justify his signature on the lockplate, and was quite happy for them to be sold as examples of his work. There is certainly no suggestion that they were engraved elsewhere, and it may well be that Twigg himself had very little to do personally with the manufacture of his weapons, even on his own premises, and I consider that such pistols should be accepted as genuine.

I purchased this pistol in 1969 from Bernard Marsh, at a time when he worked in his shop in Bridge Street, Manchester.

This gun was one of the first in my collection. It is original in all respects, with the exception of the mainspring, which has been replaced with a contemporary mainspring. Nowadays it is virtually impossible to make replacements from genuine old parts.

This weapon dates from around 1815.

Flintlock pocket pistol with barrel key. Twigg

Double-barrelled Tap Action Flintlock Pistol by Smith

SMITH, William (1810–1845)
Shop in London. Made double-barrel
fowling pieces. Also made flintlock coach
pistols and double-barrelled flintlock
overcoat pistols.

Length: 8 in.
Barrel length: $2\frac{1}{2}$ in.
Bore: 0.43 in.

This gun is a good example of the use of the tap to make two shots possible, from one loading. The barrels are unscrewed in order to load, using the shaped end of the bullet-mould. This is inserted into the muzzle, which is star-shaped in order to receive it. Once the barrels have been unscrewed, the breeches are exposed, and filled with black powder. The ball is placed on top, and the barrels screwed into position. The gun is placed on half-cock, the tap brought down to the vertical position, and the pan primed. The tap is now brought to the horizontal position, and the pan primed once more. The frizzen is then closed, the weapon fully cocked, and fired. It is then cocked again, and the tap brought down to the vertical, exposing the powder from the first priming.

The frizzen is closed, and the weapon is ready to fire again. While all this sounds very complicated, in fact the mechanism is ingenious yet quite simple, and the technique is soon learned.

This flintlock pistol is in beautiful condition and has no replacement parts. The frame of the boxlock mechanism is engraved with trophies of arms, including a terrestrial globe, pole arms, a drum, and flags. Original blueing is present between the barrels, where age and damp have been unable to penetrate. The cock is of the throat-hole type commonly found in boxlock pistols. The stock is of polished walnut, and has an oval silver escutcheon inlet behind the top strap. The barrels are numbered 1 and 2 respectively, with corresponding numbering of the breeches. Engraving consists of 'Smith', in old English script, on the left of the frame, with 'London' on the right, while the muzzles of both barrels have darted engraving around their circumferences. Proof marks are stamped on the frame and both barrels, and are of post-1813 Birmingham type. Special features of the weapon are the folding trigger, which springs down when the weapon is placed at full cock, and the sliding top safety. This engages on the back of the cock, while at the same time a peg locates in a hole at the bottom of the closed frizzen as an added protection.

Double-barrelled flintlock pocket pistol by W. Smith. Note the tap on the side of the frame, and the pincer bullet mould, with its short arm for unscrewing the barrel

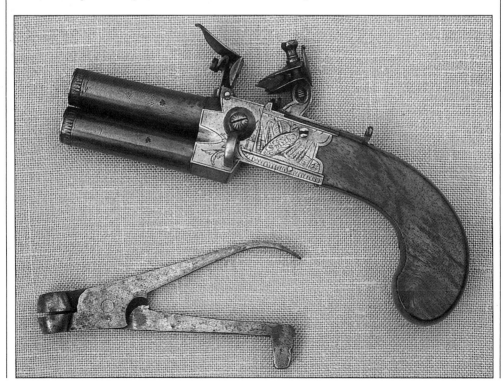

Flintlock Coach Pistol by Wilbraham

WILBRAHAM, George (1815–1854)
Shop in London. Made flintlock pocket
pistols and coach pistols. Also made
fowling pieces. Later made percussion
pistols and shotguns. His son John
carried on the business from 1854 to
1860.

Length: 13 in.	
Barrel length: 8¼ in.	
Bore: 0.56 in.	

This is a fine example of a brass-barrelled flintlock coach pistol. Only the cock, top-jaw and screw are replacements, but they are in complete harmony with the rest of the pistol, and the action is beautifully crisp. The lock and cock are of flat-section, the frizzen elongated and well shaped. The pan itself is oval in shape, and is clearly defined. The stock is of walnut, full stocked to the muzzle, and is hockey-stick in shape, without any chequering on the butt. The ramrod is a replacement which I have made myself. Unfortunately I did not use cast brass, so the colour match is not as good as I would have wished, but from a practical viewpoint it is an excellent fit, and blends well with the rest of the pistol. It incorporates a worm and brass cap, for extracting the ball. The barrel is rounded, and is not swamped.

The furniture is of brass, the trigger-guard having a pineapple finial, and engraving consists of the maker's name in Roman lettering on the lockplate, while 'London' is engraved on the barrel. A floral motif is engraved on the trigger-guard, and a sunburst on the top-jaw matches a similar one on the lockplate below the pan. Proof marks are of post-1813 Birmingham type.

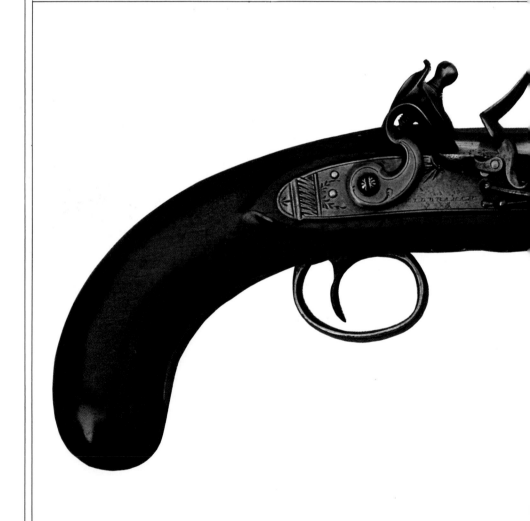

A special feature of this weapon is the roller bearing attached to the toe of the frizzen spring, to ensure a smoother action.

When I purchased this pistol, which dates from about 1820, in the early days of my collecting, it was not at all in the condition to which it has now been restored.

I well remember calling at my old friend Fred Tomlinson's one morning, in his previous premises in Wellington Road, Stockport. Without a word he handed me a bundle wrapped in several old newspapers. Inside was this pistol, which had come from a dealer in Liverpool.

The gun had, in those days, been lightened, and the stock was bleached almost white. Someone, possibly a child, had attacked it, and it was riddled with thirty or forty nail holes. These holes had to be filled in the usual way, with a mixture of walnut sawdust and strong adhesive. The stock was then sanded down, stained, and finally laboriously polished by the application of linseed oil, employed in the traditional way – a small amount of boiled linseed oil is placed in the palm of the hand and rubbed hard into the stock until it becomes hot, and this is repeated for about five or ten minutes twice daily.

After about a month the polishing was completed, and the stock remains, to this day, a highly polished surface that enhances the mellow colour of the brasswork.

The damage inflicted in past years can now scarcely be detected.

Brass-barrelled flintlock pistol by Wilbraham

Flintlock Holster Pistol by King

KING, J. (1740–1790)
Shop in London. Made screw cannon-barrel pocket pistols, and brass-barrel flintlock blunderbusses. Also muskets with Royal Cypher, and brass-barrel flintlock holster pistols.

Length: 14 in.
Barrel length: 8 in.
Bore: 0.6 in.

This superb mid-eighteenth-century flintlock holster pistol has a brass swamped barrel which is beautifully engraved. All parts are original, including the brass-tipped ramrod, which incorporates a worm at one end. The lock and cock are of the rounded variety, the lockplate being of brass. There is no bridle to the frizzen, this being secured by a single screw, while inside the lock there is no bridle to the tumbler. The stock is of walnut, and is of the 'ball-butt' variety, terminating in a grotesque mask butt-cap. The furniture, including the butt-cap, trigger-guard, sideplate and shield-shaped escutcheon, are all constructed of brass. The trigger-guard terminates in a husk finial, while the plain and slightly fretted sideplate terminates in acanthus foliage. Scroll-shaped silver wiring has been inlet around the barrel tang, ending in a shell pattern at this point. Engraving on this pistol comprises the maker's name, engraved in Roman lettering on the lockplate. There is delicate scroll engraving on the cock as well as on the tail of the lock, and a chequered pattern is engraved on the trigger-guard. Proof marks are of the early Birmingham private type.

The absence of a bridle on both the frizzen and tumbler signify that this weapon is probably slightly earlier than the Clarkson pistol described next.

The frizzen has not the elegant shape of that of the Clarkson pistol, and the frizzen spring, while perfectly functional, does not have the beautiful lines of its Clarkson counterpart. Nevertheless, the weapon is extremely well proportioned, the rounded brass lock, brass barrel and furniture being perfectly offset by the dark walnut stock.

The sideplate, too, is plainer than the rococo sideplate of the Clarkson, but the pistol as a whole is a fine weapon and extremely elegant, its brasswork contrasting sharply with the silver mounts of the Clarkson weapon.

Incidentally, the muzzle of this gun shows considerable wear at the top, due to oft-repeated drawing and replacing of the weapon into its saddle holster.

Brass-barrelled flintlock pistol by King

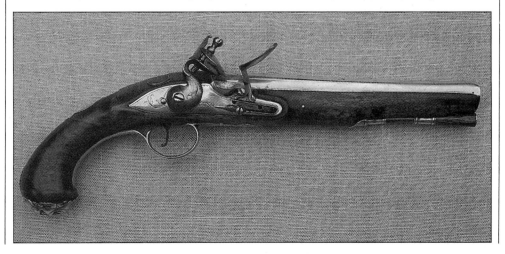

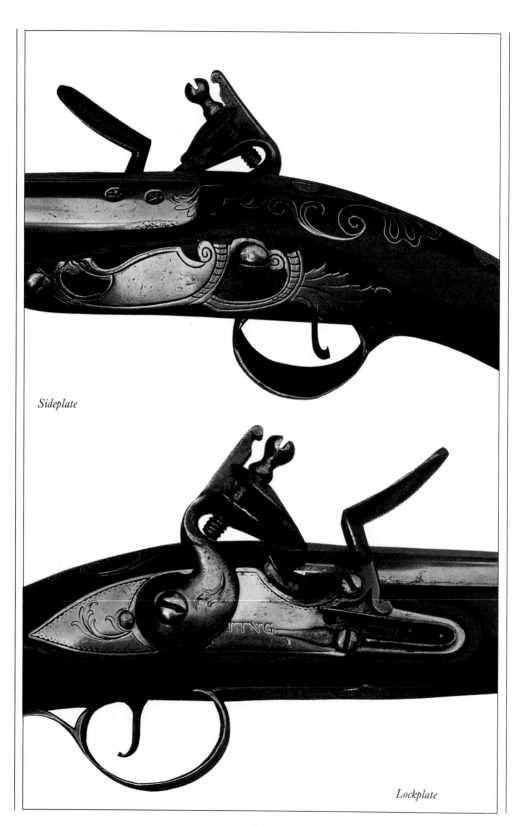

Sideplate

Lockplate

Flintlock Coach Pistol by Clarkson

CLARKSON, I. (1680–1748)
Shop in London. Made silver-mounted
flintlock holster and pocket pistols. Also
made Queen Anne boxlock flintlock
coach pistols, and had Royal
Government contract for flintlock
musket and coach pistols.

Length: 13 in.
Barrel length: 8 in.
Bore: 0.65 in.

This silver-mounted coach pistol has the same elegant classic lines as the King pistol described earlier.

The lockplate and cock are of flat section. The lower part of the frizzen is hollowed out near the vent in order to allow the powder to be packed around it, making ignition more certain. This is an added refinement which one would expect from a maker of this eminence. The walnut stock is of the 'ball-butt' variety and is of high quality. There is an old but expertly performed repair to the fore-end. There are teardrop finials behind the tail of the lock and sideplate, and silver wiring has been inlet into the stock in a scroll pattern behind the barrel tang. The ramrod is a well-made replacement, and has no worm. The barrel has an appearance known as 'watered steel', due to its mode of construction, and is slightly swamped at the muzzle. The silver mounts are particularly fine. The butt-cap is of the 'lion and rampart' type, and is silver hallmarked for the year 1747. The sideplate is of the fretted and foliate variety, and is beautifully executed. The silver escutcheon is rococo in styling, and quite magnificent. The trigger-guard is of steel, and terminates in a husk finial. Engraving consists of 'Clarkson' on the lockplate in Roman lettering and 'London' on the barrel breech. There is delicate scroll engraving to the cock and tail of the lock. The trigger-guard is engraved with an ovoid pattern. Proof marks are clearly stamped on the left side of the breech, and are of the post-1702 London type. A crowned 'F' indicates the construction of the barrel after 1741.

This weapon is in excellent condition, and with its silver mounts and high-quality stock presents a very splendid appearance. It is of the period 1740–1750, which is my favourite period for flintlock pistols, and a time when such weapons had a most elegant and well-balanced design.

Right: *Fretted silver sideplate*

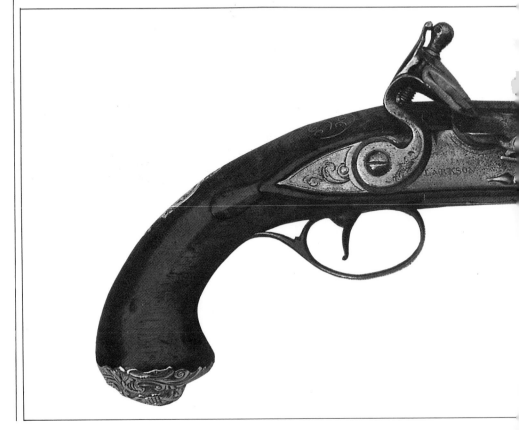

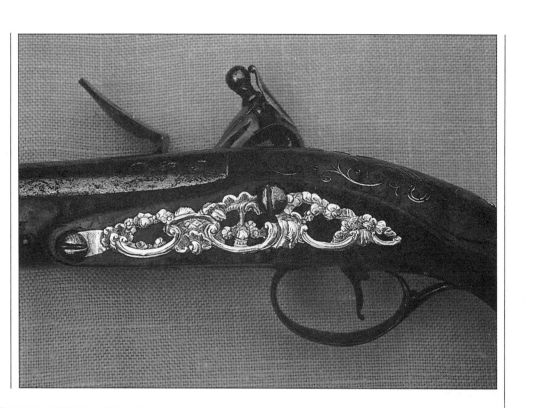

Flintlock coach pistol by Clarkson

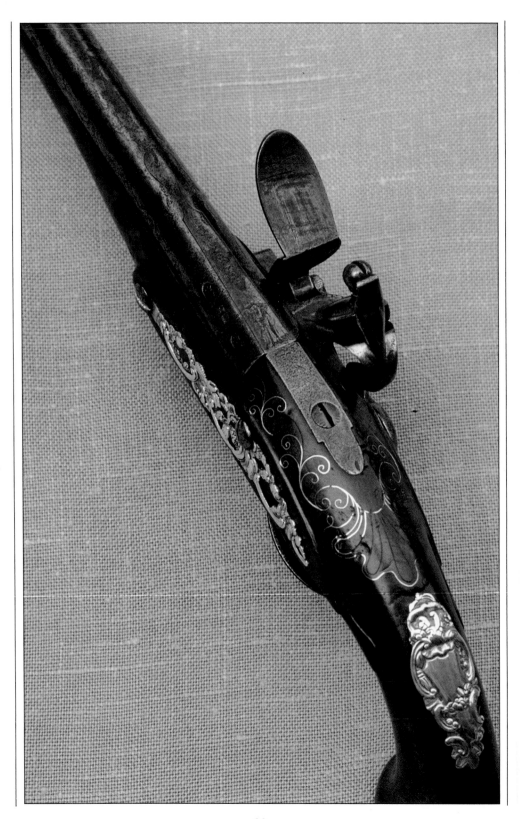

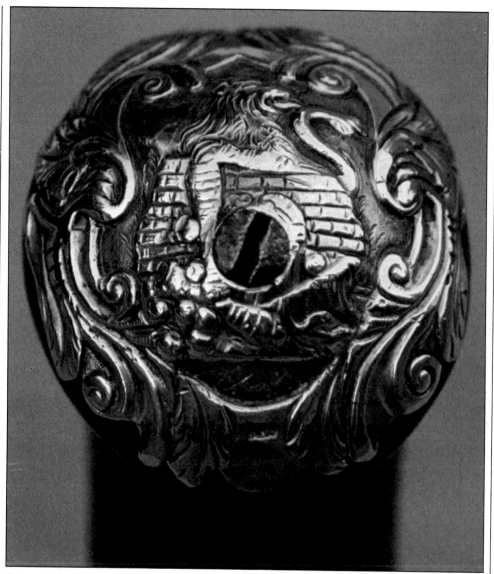

'Lion and Rampart' butt-cap

Left: *Top view of Clarkson pistol, showing watered steel barrel*

Cased Percussion
Pistols

Length: 7 in.
Barrel length: 2½ in.
Bore: 0.41 in.

This pair of silver-mounted pocket pistols are cased in their original red velvet-lined mahogany case, with a brass escutcheon in the lid. There is no trade label. The weapons are in virtually original condition, the octagonal barrels retaining most of their original blueing. The guns themselves are boxlock, with centre-swung hammers, which are in the form of engraved dolphins. There is a folding trigger. The walnut stocks are delicately chequered, the butts being bag-shaped in outline. The frames and mounts are of silver and there is a plain rectangular escutcheon inlet into the stock behind the barrel tang, and a silver butt-cap is fitted. Engraving of scroll form is present on each side of the frame, and on the top strap, the muzzles having darted engraving, while the butt-cap is engraved with a sunburst. Proof marks of post-1813 Birmingham type are stamped on the barrels and frames. The weapons are encased together with several accessories, including a delightful and tiny pistol flask with a beautiful patina, stamped 'Sykes', an ebony-handled turnscrew, a powder measure, several balls, a bullet mould, percussion caps, a combined nipple and barrel key, and a nipple box containing two original nipples.

It can be seen that one of the weapons is slightly more worn than the other, but there is a very good reason for this.

Some years ago, a Buxton antique dealer went to a house in Derbyshire to see an old dresser. On opening a drawer he discovered the more worn of the two pistols, and asked if he could buy it. The owner declined, saying that somewhere or other there was another pistol in a box, and, if she ever came across it, she would bring the two guns in to the dealer. In the course of time this is what actually happened – the guns were delivered to the dealer, who then sold them to my old contact, Fred Tomlinson.

Unfortunately, however, having recently made another purchase, I was not in any position to add further to my collection, and accordingly had to let the opportunity pass.

At that time, I should add, the only accessories in the case consisted of the percussion caps, the ball mould, and a dozen or so lead balls.

For many months thereafter I bitterly regretted not having purchased these guns, and I even began to dream about them, which is rather remarkable, but it does indicate that I felt drawn to them in some inexplicable way. Imagine my delight, therefore, after about eighteen months, while I was exhibiting at an Arms Fair in Stockport, when I saw the guns once again, on one of the stands. Although now much dearer, the beautiful and rare flask already described was neatly fitted into its tiny compartment, and an original and contemporary turnscrew had been added, and I was delighted to be able to make the purchase, especially since one of the foremost dealers in the country was simultaneously trying to purchase the weapons from an assistant on the stand!

After many months of patient searching, I was finally able to secure the necessary barrel key, although this had to be enlarged in order to fit the guns. The delightful lignum vitae nipple box was found in an antique shop in Knutsford, and the powder measure added at a later date.

Accessories compiled in this way, in my opinion, can only enhance the value and appearance of the cased set. It is, of course, essential that the items added are original ones, and contemporary with the weapons. Also, such additions can only be made by someone who has spent years in the study of cased sets, and has the specialist knowledge necessary to decide what particular accessories would be suitable.

Overleaf: *These pistols lack any maker's name, yet are of obvious quality*

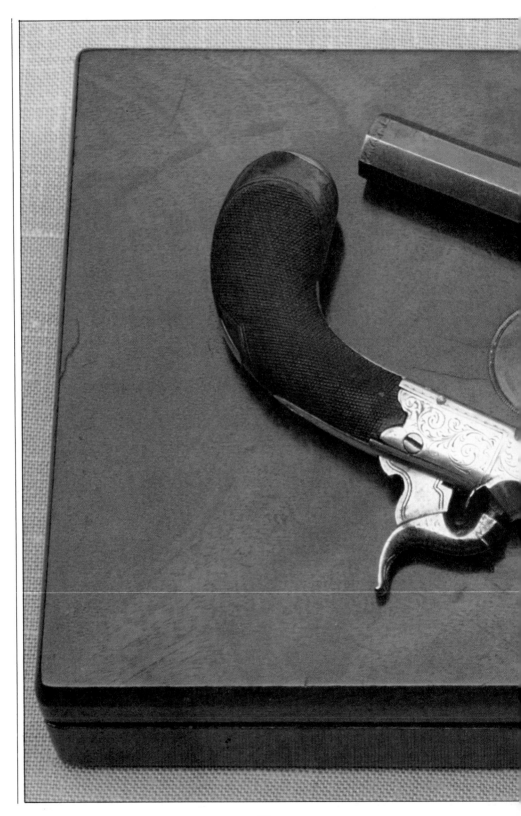

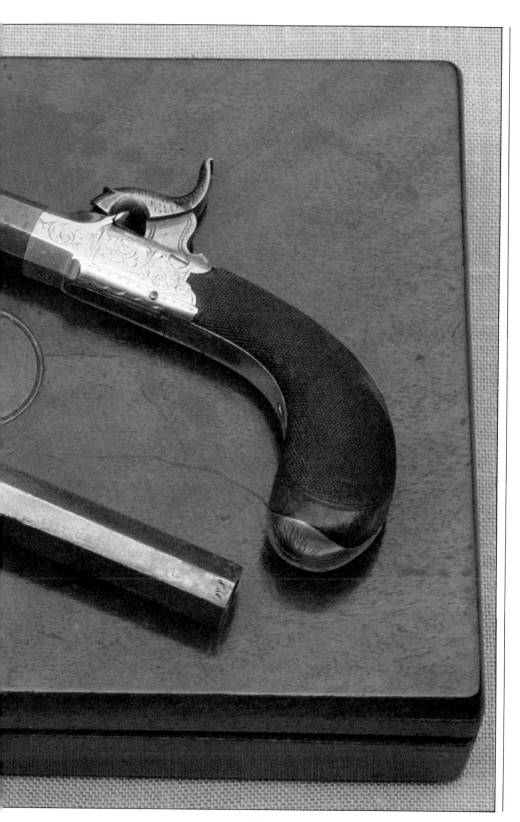

Cooper's Ring Trigger Pepperbox and Pepperbox Revolver by Horsley

COOPER, J. R. (1840–1853)
Shop in Birmingham. Patented a
percussion pepperbox in 1842.

HORSLEY, Thomas (1834–1880)
Shop at York. Made boxlock pocket
pistols with percussion locks, and
percussion pepperboxes. Also made
double-barrel pinfire shotguns.

These weapons represent the earliest attempts to produce a practical revolver, which had become a more feasible proposition with the invention of the percussion system.

Even in the matchlock era, attempts had been made to produce a rotating cylinder comprising several separate chambers, and Elisha Collier had invented a flintlock weapon with a rotating cylinder, but the discovery of the percussion cap by Joshua Shaw in the 1820s made it less possible for the charge to spread to all the chambers at once, which was a hazard associated with previous attempts.

The pepperbox comprised a single-barrel block, drilled, usually, with six separate chambers. The nipples were normally arranged coaxially, and the weapon was fired by means of a bar hammer on the top strap.

Pepperboxes, or pepperpots, as they were sometimes called, derived their name from their so-called resemblance to that household article.

COOPER'S RING TRIGGER PEPPERBOX

This was my first pepperbox, made to J. R. Cooper's patent. Cooper was a Birmingham gunmaker who copied, and improved on, a Belgian patent revolver called a Mariette. His pepperboxes had six chambers, an ingenious underhammer firing mechanism and a ring-shaped trigger.

I bought this weapon from Bernard Marsh in my early collecting days, being inspired by a photograph in Lister's textbook, which I had read many times, and which had become my 'Bible'. Lister was already an old man when I met him as a fellow member of the Northern Branch of the Arms and Armour Society. I told him how much I enjoyed reading his book, and had relied on it implicitly in the early days. He was very enthusiastic, and delighted in telling me about his cased pocket Colt revolver, which was illustrated in his book, and which he had acquired for ten shillings.

The pepperbox was quite worn, but, following my normal practice on purchasing any antique weapon, I had stripped it down to all of its component parts, so that each part could be cleaned, oiled and repaired if necessary, and finally reassembled.

Stripping an antique gun is by no means an easy task. Many of the screws can be rusted in or the slots worn, and one has to use a great deal of ingenuity in order to remove them. The first essential is a set of good screwdrivers of varying sizes. Release oil, of course, works wonders, although the parts may have to be soaked for several days. Heat can burn away old oil and release most stubborn screws, but if the weapon has any original finish, application of heat would destroy this forever. The screw slot may have to be deepened by scoring with a sharp point or knife file, to assist in its removal. Very often, in antique weapons which have lain neglected for years, the engraving can be so filled in with old oil, polish, dirt and rust, that all detail is obliterated, and by painstaking work with the point of a pin, such engraving can be cleaned out, and I have often been absolutely astonished by the amount of detail revealed by such a simple expedient.

A good example of J. R. Cooper's patent pepperbox, with ring trigger and bag-shaped grips

On one occasion, a patient of mine with an interest in antiques, who knew of my hobby, came in to see me at my surgery with a J. R. Cooper patent pepperbox. It was in pristine condition. The barrels presented an overall blackened appearance, due, presumably, to the ageing process affecting the original blueing. Only the partitions between the nipples – which in the case of the Cooper are directly behind the barrel block – were damaged, where someone had deliberately bent them with a hammer.

A small chip was missing from the walnut, bag-shaped grips. This was easily repaired by splicing a piece of similar walnut into place, sanding, smoothing and whiskering the wood, before staining to match the rest of the stock. Finally the new piece was polished to blend in with the old, so that the joint could afterwards be seen only with difficulty.

The partitions were easily knocked back into shape again.

Some years ago, I acquired my present pepperbox. This weapon is in very fine condition, and is by Horsley of York.

PEPPERBOX REVOLVER BY HORSLEY

This pistol has a revolving barrel block with six chambers. There is a bar hammer on the top strap, the nipples being arranged coaxially. It has a flared walnut butt, which is finely chequered, with a butt trap in the base to accommodate percussion caps. The lid of the butt trap is engraved with a flower of the daisy family.

The barrels retain most of their original case hardening, and the top strap has its original blueing. This is a brilliant kingfisher blue, and in my opinion cannot be equalled, or mimicked, by present-day gunsmiths. Even the screws of this weapon are beautifully and delicately engraved.

Proof and view marks are of the London type, and are stamped alternately on the fluting between each chamber. The frame of the pistol is entirely covered in scroll engraving. One side is engraved 'T. Horsley, York,' in Roman lettering. On the opposite side is engraved 'Improved Revolving Pistol'.

The silver escutcheon has an 'S' surmounted by a coronet engraved upon it, indicating that it was formerly in the possession of a Duke. Unfortunately, however, the question of its original ownership remains open, as reference to Fairbairn's Crests reveals a number of possibilities.

This pistol dates from around 1850. Gold had been discovered in California at Sutter's Mill in 1849, and hordes of prospectors poured into California in the hope of finding that precious metal. It is said that the favoured sidearm amongst the 'fortyniners', as they were called, was the pepperbox revolver, because of its multishot capacity and speed of action.

Bar hammer pepperbox by T. Horsley of York

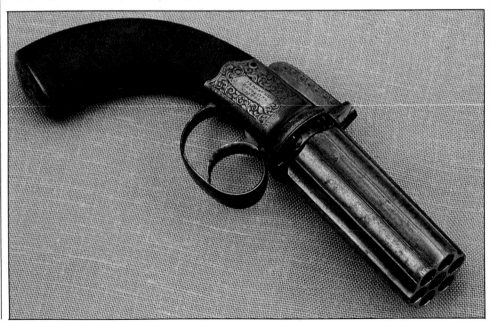

'Spanish Charlie' Cased Colt Navy Revolver (1851)

COLT, Samuel (1836–1860)
Patented percussion revolver in 1836.
Opened factory at Paterson, New Jersey.
Factory moved to Hartford, Connecticut,
1849. In 1851 exhibited at Great
Exhibition; opened London factory at
Pimlico in 1853. Models produced were
Army, Navy, Walker, Dragoon, Pocket,
Paterson, Roots, Police and Derringer.

This weapon has a barrel length of 7½ inches and a calibre of 0.36 in. It has an overall blackened appearance due to the effects of rusting and age. This kind of finish can be produced artificially, but is absolutely authentic on this pistol.

The serial number 12044 is shared by all parts of the gun, with the exception of the cylinder, which is numbered 11919. This number is so close to that on the rest of the weapon that I am convinced that it was supplied as a spare with the original set and, as often happened, had to be replaced during the working life of the pistol.

The cylinder scene is intact, and consists of a naval battle – in fact, the U.S.S. *Mississippi* in action. The W. L. Ormsby signature is too faint to be deciphered – this was the name of Colt's engraver.

This weapon is six shot. It has ivory grips, which are a beautiful mellow colour, rather than the standard issue walnut grips.

The gun is cased in its original mahogany case, with deep red velvet lining. The case had been slightly damaged, but is now repaired. The layout is of American styling, being entirely different from London casing.

I purchased this gun early on in my collecting career from Fred Tomlinson. It had actually been sold before I saw it, to a collector of clocks and Morgan sports cars, but when he heard how keen I was to purchase the gun, being appreciative of the feelings of a fellow collector he nobly and generously changed his mind, and allowed me to make the purchase.

When I first saw the case, it contained only the gun, and a small receptacle with a handle. This latter I threw away, failing totally to recognize, in my state of knowledge at that time, that this was, in fact, an accessory used to facilitate the heating of lead before casting lead ball, and was, in all probability, contemporary with the case and revolver.

It was several months before I managed to obtain a bullet mould of the correct size, stamped 'Colt's Patent', and capable of casting conical or round bullets. It was, however, several years before I purchased the correct cap tin for the weapon, having experimented with several others. Finally the correct japanned box, stamped 'Eley London' was obtained, and placed in the case in the appropriate compartment. Once the mould had been obtained, it was very easy to cast a few balls, and age them to make them appear contemporary with the case.

Several years ago, I was fortunate in obtaining an original Colt Navy mainspring, but I have as yet failed to acquire an original Colt nipple key/turnscrew. I have made one myself, and had another made for me, but neither is quite perfect, and nowadays it is easier to find gold than original Colt nipple keys.

The powder flask was a different problem. Colt was prepared to supply any flask to the customer's orders. The standard type is known as the Colt Navy flask, having an embossed stand of arms on one side, and incorporating a cannon and Colt's Patent stamp. It has a sloping charger to facilitate loading. These were made by the American Flask and Cap Company. The flask encased with the gun is the only one I have been able to find which is remotely suitable. It has the correct sloping charger, sometimes known as the Navy charger. This flask was also made by the American Flask and Cap Company, and was normally supplied for Remington revolvers. It is known as the 'Wreath, Dog, and Birds' flask, and is thus contemporary with the Colt, and might easily have been

Colt Navy percussion revolver. Note ivory grips

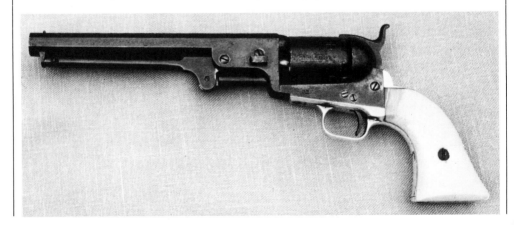

38

specified by the original customer.

The box of unopened skin cartridges is designed for the Colt Police revolver. This weapon is also of 36 calibre, and so is quite suitable for use with the Colt Navy revolver.

The story of Samuel Colt is a fascinating one, and epitomizes the American dream. He was the inventor of the first practical revolver, and was the first person to introduce the production line into the firearms industry. All the major parts of his guns were stamped with a serial number, matching numbers being then assembled by relatively unskilled labour. His revolvers had few working parts, and were therefore very robust. The barrels were rifled, and this made them very accurate, more accurate, in fact, than the existing musket of the day.

Rifling is a series of parallel grooves, cut into the bore of the weapon in a slow spiral, in order to impart spin to the bullet, thus emulating a principle which had been established by the early arrow makers, who inserted the feathers in their arrows in such a way as to impart spin, thereby increasing their accuracy, and this principle was applied to the firearms industry.

Colt's first factory was opened in Paterson, New Jersey, in 1836. His new revolver was not a particular success, but following the Mexican War of 1846 his revolver was redesigned, culminating in the opening of a new factory, in Hartford, Connecticut, in 1849. This factory is still in existence.

The Colt Navy revolver in my collection has a particular history of its own, which was given to me on the purchase of the gun. This relates that 'The gun was once the property of a man called Charles Wilson, who was nicknamed "Spanish Charlie". He was once the mate of a slave ship, who died in St Helena in the early years of this century. He used to refer to the slaves as "so many cattle", and invariably treated them as such. In the event of any undue clamour in that part of the vessel occupied by the slaves, he used to present this weapon through a hole in the bulkhead, and fire two rounds from it into their midst. Such treatment, he stated, never failed to quieten and subdue them.'

And we are not surprised to learn this.

The Colt Navy revolver was the most popular of Colt's percussion revolvers and was used extensively by both sides during the American Civil War. It is said that Wild Bill Hickok wore two of these guns, which were holstered butt foremost, in order to facilitate the cross draw which was popular on the American frontier at that time.

Overleaf: *Accessories cased with Colt Navy revolver*

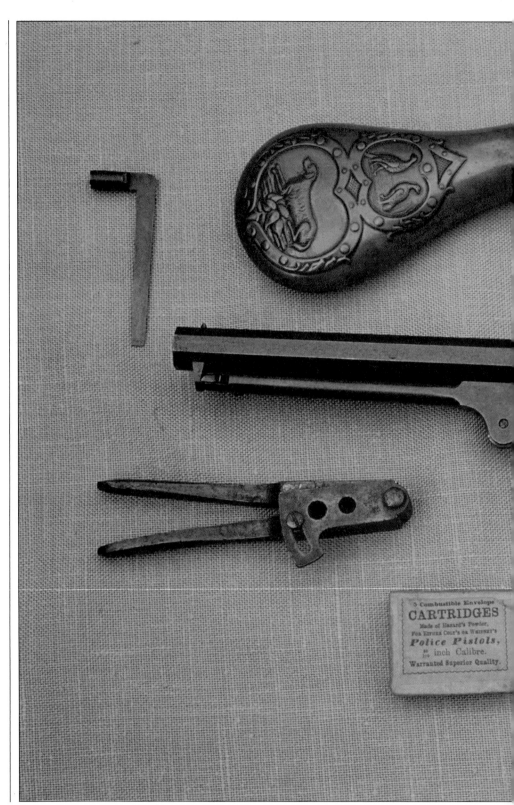

Derringers

In May 1970, I was holidaying with my family on the Island of Ibiza. One afternoon we decided to take a bus trip to a beach on another part of the island, and somewhere in the hills, the bus stopped to disgorge its passengers at an antique shop. In the gardens there were several ancient amphorae. Inside the shop there was the usual heavy Spanish furniture, and several old percussion pistols of little merit. Also on display were a few pistols with enormous double barrels, which dropped down either by sliding the trigger guard to one side or by operating a lever on the top strap. These guns were to be found all over Spain at that time, and were probably cut down double-barrelled shotguns.

I strolled around casually, and, happening to look upwards, noted the muzzle of an over-and-under double-barrelled pistol peeping out over the edge of the shelf. My heart leaped – this could only be a derringer, the sort of gun used by gamblers, or worn by dance-hall girls in their garters in downbeat Western films.

With trembling hand, I reached up and brought the gun down. It was exactly as I'd thought, a Remington 0.41 calibre over-and-under derringer, in very rusty condition, with the hammer spur broken off. On the upper barrel flat was engraved 'E. Remington & Sons, Ilion, N.Y.'.

I purchased this gun for the princely sum of £7. Now this was long before hand luggage was subjected to X-ray techniques to detect firearms at airport terminals, and in view of the gun's general poor and broken condition, I thought that there was little likelihood of my being refused permission to bring it into the country. However, not wishing to test this theory too far, I thrust the gun to the bottom of my hand luggage, grabbed another heavy suitcase with one hand, and with a child on the other, and an easily conjured up, if not habitual, harassed look familiar to all parents of young children, I blustered my way through the green door.

The gun was quite badly pitted in places, and the action rusted solid, but weeks of patient work restored the metalwork, and the mechanism, after years of abuse and disuse, was again smoothly oiled and functional.

I copied the spur from a photograph, filing the shape out of solid steel, and had it welded on and engraved with delicate cross-hatching.

Some years later, in a moment of ridiculous panic, since all breech-loading cartridge weapons require a Firearms Certificate, I hurled this weapon off the pier at Largs, where I believe it must still lie. This was totally ignoring a legal precedent that allows such firearms to be kept provided they are kept purely as antiques. I would certainly not have liked to fire this gun at any time, as I am sure it would have blown up in my hand.

A few years ago, another derringer came into my possession. This was a contemporary copy of a Sharp's 0.22 calibre four-barrelled derringer. It was a most beautiful weapon. The barrels had their original blackened finish, known as charcoal blueing. The frame was of bronze, and was entirely covered in delicate scroll engraving. The grips were missing when I purchased the weapon, but I had new grips made in ivory. These were somewhat rough and poorly shaped, but careful work with sandpaper and polish produced perfectly smooth and highly polished grips of fine shape, which blended well with the magnificent bronze of the frame and blackening of the barrels. After a few months, and without any artificial aids, the ivory had become a mellow colour, with the appearance of great age, in keeping with the age of the weapon itself.

In the course of time, I obtained a mahogany box of just the right size. This I lined with red velvet, and fitted it with compartments in the same manner and style as the originals, including two triangular lids of mahogany with artificially aged ivory studs. With my lathe I manufactured a tiny turnscrew with an ebony handle. I also made several dummy 0.22 cartridges, with lead bullets. At a later date I added a tiny original cleaning rod, and the outfit was complete.

However, in this case also, I decided that this cartridge weapon should not form part of my collection, and I reluctantly parted with it.

The legendary gunfighter, Wild Bill Hickok, owned a Sharp's four-barrelled derringer, and was so fond of this weapon that, following his murder during a poker game in 1876, the gun was buried with him. Following pressure from collectors several years ago, his remains were disinterred, and the derringer recovered. It has now been preserved for posterity in an American museum.

Flintlock Blunderbuss by Probin

PROBIN, Thomas (1700–1780)
Shop in London. Two generations.
Made flintlock duelling and holster
pistols. Also made flintlock
blunderbusses and fowling pieces.

Length: 2 ft. 6 in.
Barrel length: 14½ in.
Bore: 1.38 in.

One evening when I had gone to bed fairly early, the telephone rang, at about 11.30 p.m. It was my old friend Fred Tomlinson. He had just purchased a small collection of antique weapons, and invited me over to inspect them. I was up and dressed within a few minutes, which makes me suspect that this was more than ten years ago, since my reactions today are somewhat slower. I was soon sitting on the floor of his lounge examining a remarkable collection of antique guns.

There were two Scottish Doune pistols, a blunderbuss, a magnificent Japanese matchlock, an Unwin and Rodgers knife pistol, a pair of flintlock pocket pistols by Archer and several others of equal merit.

However, it was the blunderbuss that I wanted, and that I carried away with me when I left in the small hours. The blunderbuss was by Thomas Probin of London, a very famous London gunsmith. It had a brass barrel and the mechanism was flintlock. The buttplate and sideplate were also of brass. The walnut stock was highly polished and in superb condition. The lock was flat in section, with the maker's name engraved in script upon it. The ramrod was original, but minus its worm, which I replaced at a later date.

Other than careful cleaning and oiling, the weapon required no repair work of any kind, being in original condition throughout. Proof marks were early London in type.

Some blunderbusses have a spring bayonet, which folds, either beneath the barrel or above it. Iron-barrelled versions do exist, but are less attractive.

There are two misconceptions regarding blunderbusses that I would like to correct. The first is, that they were loaded with anything handy – rusty nails, bolts, stones, or pieces of broken glass. This was not the case. They were invariably loaded with twenty or thirty lead balls. Secondly, it was believed that the flared muzzle helped to spread the charge over a wider area. Modern ballistics experts tell us, however, that the spread of the shot is related to the narrowest part of the bore, not the widest, a phenomenon known as windage.

Blunderbusses sometimes have inscriptions engraved around the muzzle, for example, 'For Her Majesty's Mail Coaches', or, 'Happy He, Who Escapes Me', and if you haven't got such an inscription on your weapon, there are certain unscrupulous people who would be only too happy to put one there for you. It is the old story of *caveat emptor* – let the buyer beware.

I believe that blunderbusses were seldom fired in anger. After all, it would take a very brave man indeed to argue with two inches of muzzle thrust into his face. They were, however, ideal weapons for protection, either at home or in the coach, and four-poster beds sometimes contained compartments to conceal the family 'protector'.

Pocket Colt Revolver

I have had three pocket Colts throughout my years of collecting antique guns. The first was a four-inch barrel American pocket Colt. Round the cylinder was engraved a stagecoach hold-up scene, but only traces remained. All serial numbers matched – 138262.

This weapon was made in four-, five-, and six-inch barrel sizes, 1848 being the first year of production of the early models.

I can remember going to a house auction south of Macclesfield. An old man had died and, after his death, this gun had been found lying in a drawer. I spent a whole morning at the auction, and to my delight, because this was my very first auction, I had the gun knocked down to me for £80.

The gun had an overall dark patina that I felt it best to remove. The action was, however, quite perfect, although the gun itself showed some evidence of wear.

Two years ago I acquired my present pocket Colt. It, too, had a four-inch barrel. It had been in the possession of a lady who was then moving house. The gun was in its original case, which was rather dirty and separating at its joints. All the partitions, as well as the velvet base lining, were missing. The accessories were all present, however, with the exception of the powder flask. The lid lining and that on the sides of the base was still intact, as was the shaped lining below the bullet mould.

The lady had told the dealer who had bought the gun originally that the flask had been knocking about the house until recently, but although she searched the house high and low, and was offered a substantial sum for the flask should it ever turn up, no trace of it was ever found – unfortunately it must have been thrown out with the removal rubbish.

This flask is an extremely rare one, and is of the type known as 'Eagle and Stars'. Tracing an original is marginally more difficult than finding the proverbial needle in a haystack. However, the search goes on.

The weapon is in fine condition. It is 0.31 in. calibre and has the two-line New York address on the top of the octagonal barrel. The cylinder is five-chambered. It has seven-grooved rifling, in common with all Colt revolvers.

All serial numbers match, including the wedge. The original case hardening on the entire frame and cylinder is still intact, and some blueing is still in evidence on the loading lever and environs, but is now absent from the barrel itself.

The stagecoach scene on the cylinder is complete. Apart from the flask the accessories are intact, and include the original blued nipple key/turnscrew, an Eley Bros. cap tin, a few conical bullets, Colt's Patent stamped bullet mould with its original case hardening, and the case key. The flask is a contemporary one, and will suffice until the correct replacement can be found.

The first task to be completed was the careful cleaning and regluing of the case itself. When finished, the transformation was quite remarkable, the gleaming mahogany box enhancing the external appearance of the whole outfit.

Next, it was necessary to obtain worn velvet of the correct thickness. New velvet would be useless, as it had to blend with the velvet remaining in the case, and I wanted to preserve what was original at all costs.

Next, the material had to be dyed to exactly the shade of the old. This was a laborious process which took many weeks to achieve, but finally, any

Bullet mould for Colt revolver, showing its capacity to mould round or conical ball

difference in colour or texture between the two materials was barely distinguishable.

I then made a study of photographs of cased Colts of all types, in order to find out *exactly* how the gun had been cased, since it was impossible, due to the absence of lining in the base, to determine from pressure marks and/or staining marks the position of the various items.

It was Samuel Colt's practice to case individual guns according to the prospective client's requirements. Thus it was soon evident to me that this gun had been cased on a 'one-off' basis, because in all my researches I could not find a single example of such a neat casing, the box size being no larger than the gun encased within it.

Consequently, using the outline of the mould base which was still present as one parameter, and with the gun in the only position available, I was able to work out the only possible situations of the various partitions. These were then constructed from softwood, sanded to a taper, covered in material, and inserted into the correct positions.

Pressure marks were then created to give the appearance of the various items having lain *in situ* for some considerable time. Following this, rust marks were then included, to match similar marks in the lid lining, and a little oil in the correct places soon created the desired effect of age. In this connection it must be said that there is no intention to deceive when casing in this way. The whole appearance of this set has been transformed by replacing the velvet lining. To do so with, say, a new piece of lining, would create wholly the wrong effect. For the set to *look* authentic it must be made to *be* authentic. This gun cost no less for being in a damaged case. But now the whole set is enhanced by its aura of originality.

Close-up view of pocket Colt cylinder

English Pocket Colt

While regularly attending the monthly meetings of the Northern Branch of the Arms and Armour Society, I became friendly with a fellow member who had a London Colt.

Samuel Colt came to London in 1851, to the Great Exhibition, where he displayed enormous panoplies of his new revolvers. This he did in order to publicize his invention and, hopefully, to interest the British Ordnance in purchasing his weapons. He was a marvellous entrepreneur, and liberally awarded presentation pieces to gentlemen who happened to be well placed to help his cause. To some extent he succeeded, and 4000 Navy Colts were sold to the British Navy, for use in the Crimean War. He opened a factory in Pimlico, on the banks of the Thames, in 1853, and sold mainly Navy revolvers and pocket models. Guns made in the London factory bore the London address, together with London proof marks. They were normally set up in oak cases, with completely different casing arrangements from their American counterparts. The flask was bag-shaped, and was made in England by James Dixon and Sons.

My Arms and Armour friend and I concluded a deal. This was a straight swap, his cased London pocket Colt for my Brown Bess.

Financially, as things have turned out, the deal worked out far better for him than it did for me, but this is of little consequence, since I parted with the gun a long time ago. The outfit was, however, absolutely authentic. The trade label was present in the lid, with detailed instructions for loading and cleaning the gun.

Unfortunately, however, damp had penetrated the closed gun box, destroying all of the original blueing and causing moderate pitting throughout the weapon. This I was able to remove after much work, but the gun then required to be recoloured, and this process took a great deal of time.

Thereafter, I never felt quite the same about the gun, because although it looked splendid, with a beautiful dark patination, and was crisp in every detail, it had actually lost quite a bit of metal in the filing, and I was always aware of this each time I handled it. The presence of pitting, however, is always unsightly on any weapon, but much more so on a cased item, and this is why I felt it necessary to remove this disfigurement from the gun.

Fowling Pieces

SINGLE-BARRELLED PERCUSSION SHOTGUN

Length: 3 ft. 8 in.
Barrel length: 2 ft. 3in.
Bore: 0.65 in.

This weapon has an engraved back-action lock. The metal parts, including the barrel, have an overall dark patina. The twist pattern of the barrel can be easily seen, and the walnut stock is in excellent condition.

When I purchased this longarm, the ramrod pipe was missing. This I had made, and silver-soldered on. A ramrod was then constructed by sanding an appropriate length of dowelling to the correct size. This was then stained to match the stock, and polish was applied. A horn tip was fitted at the muzzle end, and a worm and cap at the other.

SINGLE-BARRELLED PERCUSSION SHOTGUN

Length: 3 ft. 10 in.
Barrel length: 2 ft. 6in.
Bore: 0.732 in.

This weapon, too, had an engraved back-action lock, inscribed 'Mears' on the lockplate. It was purchased in the infancy of my collecting years, from a non-specialist antique shop in Glasgow. Hanging there in the shop, in the dim light well above eye level, the gun looked in pristine condition, and I paid over my £10 and proudly bore my purchase home.

When I examined it in the cold light of day, however, a very different picture emerged. The gun was in extremely poor condition, the nipple and barrel tang broken and the stock cracked across and ill-fitting. This was truly the start of my stock repair work. Weeks were spent in repairing the broken stock, in making filler, patching up, and repolishing.

Next, the old nipple had to be drilled out and a new one made and fitted. Finally, the broken parts of the barrel tang had to be welded together.

I therefore approached my friend and asked him to effect these repairs. He asked me whether the gun was loaded, and I was able to reply in the negative, as when I had been cleaning out the bore, and had inserted a ramrod and worm down the barrel, I had, in fact, ascertained that the gun was loaded, and had removed about thirty bird-shot, which I still have preserved.

My friend met me a few days later and informed me that he had nearly required my medical services. Apparently, he had fixed the gun barrel pointing downwards in his vice, but when he applied his blow-torch to the barrel tang there had been an explosion which had almost blown his foot off! I had made an elementary mistake. Fowling pieces are loaded by pouring in a powder charge, then a wad, then the shot and finally a second wad. Although I had emptied the second wad and the shot, the powder and the first wad still remained!

Once the repair had been effected and the gun reassembled, it really looked quite presentable, even in daylight, but I was still thankful to sell it for the same figure at which I'd purchased it. It had taken several tubes of epoxy resin and many hours of work, but had taught me a few lessons that I never forgot.

DOUBLE-BARRELLED PERCUSSION SHOTGUN

> **Length**: 3 ft. 10 in.
> **Barrel length**: 2 ft. 6 in.
> **Bore**: 0.70 in.

The last fowling piece to form part of my collection was a double-barrelled Spanish shotgun. One hammer was missing, the ramrod was absent, the stock in poor condition and the barrels deeply pitted. On the barrel rib was inscribed 'En Eibar', which is the town of origin of many Spanish gun barrels.

I really enjoyed working on these barrels, happily filing and sanding away in the garage, inhaling steel dust and debris, at what cost time alone will tell.

Eventually, the barrels were polished to a mirror finish, using successively finer grades of wet and dry sandpaper, finishing off with 000 steel wool.

At this stage the barrels were degreased and browned. Browning is a process of artificial rusting, which, while preventing further rusting of the barrels, also colours them in such a way as to bring out the twist method of construction, thereby enhancing the appearance of the piece. Most gun barrels were browned by applying a solution of chemical to the degreased barrels, leaving them for twelve hours and rubbing the resulting rusty deposit off again. This is repeated until, after about two weeks, a permanent brown colour is imparted, which is in, rather than on, the surface of the metal. All traces of the chemical are then removed and the barrels waxed.

The solution I use is an ancient formula, and is very effective. I had it made up to my own prescription by a chemist many years ago!

I managed to obtain a percussion hammer which more or less matched the other, and making a ramrod and tip, and a steel worm and cap, constituted fairly simple lathe operations.

The overall result was quite astounding. Here was a weapon which, to all intents and purposes, was destined for scrap, but by dint of careful restoration, a worn-out piece has not only been preserved for posterity but has in fact been brought back to something approaching its original condition.

The Gun That Never Was

In 1972, a friend of mine who knew of my interest in antique guns contacted me to tell me of a weapon that a distant relative of his, living near Dumfries, had found in her attic. She had laid the pistol down on to a large piece of paper and drawn its outline. The resulting diagram she had sent to my friend, who knew a little about firearms. In his considered opinion, this gun was a Colt revolver and, if I wished, he would contact his relative and arrange for me to see and purchase the weapon from her.

I was on tenterhooks awaiting the necessary arrangements. This gun was quite probably a Colt Navy revolver, might even be a Paterson Colt – a rare early model worth, in those days, at least £3,000. I had heard of such weapons being discovered by accident in Scotland, and was convinced that at last I was going to strike it lucky.

Anticipating a happy outcome to our meeting, I arranged a weekend, with my wife and children, in the Douglas Arms Hotel in Castle Douglas.

We duly arrived on a Friday afternoon. I hurriedly dressed for dinner and, while the family were preparing themselves for the usual splendid meal in that comfortable establishment, I drove the few miles to Dalbeattie with pounding heart.

Dalbeattie is a small Scottish town near the Solway coast composed of little granite houses amidst a background of Scotch pines. From its quarry was mined the granite from which Manchester Town Hall was built.

I knocked on the door of the tiny terraced house in the main street, and it was opened by a little old lady, who took me into the front room. It was a very poor and sparsely furnished house.

'I've come about the gun,' I said, my heart still pounding. Mentally I was thinking, 'I'll be quite happy, even if it's only a Colt Navy.'

'Oh!,' she said, 'you'll be the doctor.' She went on, 'I showed the gun to an old friend of mine (my heart sank immediately) and he says I need a certificate for it, so I've taken it to the Police Station.'

Police Station! I was stricken. All this way, and the woman had taken it to the Police Station!

Then she continued, 'If you want to, we can go along and see it there.' Suddenly I felt better again. Navy Colt, Paterson Colt even, all is not yet lost.

Together we walked the 200 or so yards to the Police Station. The desk sergeant looked up. 'Just hold on a minute, doctor, and I'll get the gun for you.' He went to the safe and pulled out an object wrapped in a white rag. My pulses were racing again as I reached out to receive the treasured object. I unwrapped it slowly.

There, in all its glory, lay a silver-plated single-shot Belgian target pistol with the hammer spur broken off. It was a cartridge weapon, and, theoretically at least, required a Firearms Certificate. To a collector like myself, it was worth . . . nothing.

'Do you want it?' asked the desk sergeant, who obviously didn't know one end of a gun from another.

'No.' I replied, 'No, thank you.'

Scottish Percussion Belt Pistol by Westley Richards

RICHARDS, William Westley, and
Westley (1812–1872)
Shop at 82 High Street, Birmingham.
Active in establishing the Birmingham
Proof House in 1813. In 1815, opened a
shop at 170 Bond Street, London.

I was fortunate enough to acquire this Scottish pistol several years ago. This type of pistol is traditionally associated with the village of Doune, in Perthshire, and, indeed, with certain families of gunsmiths, notably Cadell, Campbell and Murdoch.

Scottish pistols were normally of all-metal construction, and had a butt which was either lobe shaped, heart shaped or ramshorn shaped. With the advent of the percussion era, they were produced in Birmingham in large numbers, and were worn with the then very popular Highland Dress.

This particular pistol was by Westley Richards, and was so engraved on the lockplate.

The butt was of the ramshorn type, but the ball-shaped pricker between the horns was missing. Also absent were the steel ramrod, the hammer and the mainspring.

The entire pistol was covered in scroll engraving that was beautifully executed and intricate in design, incorporating a fawn and thistle amidst the interlacing scrollwork, and there was a belt hook on the left side of the gun. However, the features which attracted my attention were two cartouches, with mottoes inscribed around them. One had the initials 'W.F.T.', and a motto: 'Occultus non extinctus', while the other had a stag's head erased, close to a motif showing the sun's rays emerging from behind a cloud. Here was inscribed a second motto: 'Je suis prest' (*sic*).

Reference to Fairbairn's *Crests* revealed that the stag's head is the crest of the Fraser family, as is the motto 'Je suis prest' – ('I am ready'), while the sun's rays hidden behind a cloud and the motto 'Occultus non extinctus' ('Hidden, not lost'), are those of the Tytler family.

Further research yielded the information that Tytler was the name assumed by the descendants of one Seton, who killed a man accidentally and was forced to flee to France. His children returned to this country, adopted the name Tytler, and later married into the Fraser family, becoming Fraser-Tytler.

William Fraser-Tytler, to whom the initials belong, was the original owner of the gun, and had a distinguished Army career, firstly with the Bengal Army and later with the Ayrshire Volunteers.

The family seat is at Aldourie Castle, in Inverness-shire.

I have been in touch with descendants of the family, who are closely related to Cameron of Lochiel, at Aldourie Castle, and the present occupant informs me that his ancestor William was very fond of putting his crests and mottoes on all his possessions, as they have cause to regret, because of his Victorian additions to the ancient stronghold.

In the course of time, I had a ball pricker made and engraved to match the ball trigger. A ramrod of suitable style was also fabricated, and a mainspring made and tempered. Finally, a hammer was constructed, being hand filed from carbon steel. This was then engraved in intricate fashion, its style matching perfectly the engraving on the rest of the weapon.

This was undoubtedly a worthy restoration and, in my opinion, none of the restoration work was remotely detectable.

Although only indirectly responsible, I masterminded the repairs and undertook the considerable research required to establish the gun's provenance.

It is very rare indeed that one is able to ascertain the previous owner of any weapon, and I relished greatly the opportunity I was given with this Scottish pistol.

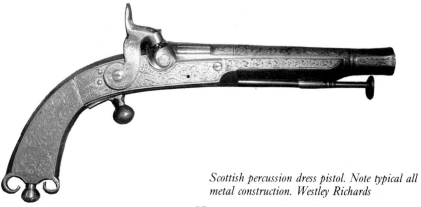

Scottish percussion dress pistol. Note typical all metal construction. Westley Richards

Tower Pistols

To the uninitiated, Tower pistols are rather ugly weapons that tend to show much evidence of hard usage. One military pistol seems very much like another, apart from a few minor differences.

However, it is these selfsame minor differences, in fact, that stimulate the collector of military pistols to purchase these particular weapons. He becomes fascinated by the different variations to be found, and although these guns do not have the quality of workmanship of firearms made for civilian use, they are nevertheless functional weapons with an intrinsic appeal of their own.

Early pistols, that is to say, up until 1764, were normally engraved with the maker's name and date across the tail of the lock, but after this time the word 'Tower', in Roman lettering, was engraved in this position.

The Royal Cypher, that is to say, the crowned initials of the sovereign – G.R., V.R., etc. – were engraved on the lockplate, together with the crown and broad arrow of the armourer's mark. The barrels were proved, firstly in the rough state, by firing a double charge of powder and ball, when the View mark was applied, usually on the left side of the breech. This consisted of a crown over the Royal Cypher, and a broad arrow.

The finished barrel was again subjected to proof, and, if successful, the Tower Proof mark was stamped below the View mark, and consisted of a crown over crossed sceptres.

There was such a demand for military weapons that the Tower alone was unable to supply sufficient arms to meet the Army's demands, so private gunsmiths in London and the provinces were commissioned to produce such weapons to specific patterns, known as sealed patterns, which were then usually sent to the Tower for proving.

Pistols were normally issued in pairs, but were never favoured as sidearms for the British soldier.

SEA-SERVICE FLINTLOCK PISTOL

Length: 19 in.
Barrel length: 12 in.
Bore: 0.56 in.

This Tower pistol is a magnificent arm. It has a 12-inch barrel, and has no stock repairs or replacement parts whatsoever. It is in pristine condition, and has the bright overall finish customary for Tower pistols.

The lockplate and cock are of flat form, while the cock is of the 'throat-hole' variety. The mainspring is very strong, and the lock action crisp and positive. The stock is of straight-grained walnut, and is stamped with a date – 1805. The ramrod is a replacement, but is of the correct pattern, having a distinct shoulder below its tip. The tip itself is of cast brass, its colour matching perfectly with the mellow brasswork of the rest of the gun furniture. The ramrod pipe, sideplate and butt-cap are of brass, the latter being of the type known as 'skullcrushing'. The lock markings are the usual ones for Tower pistols of this period – the word 'Tower' across the tail of the lock, together with the Royal Cypher – a crowned G.R., and the crown and broad arrow, which represent the armourer's mark. Proof marks appear on the left side of the breech, adjacent to another armourer's mark.

A special feature of this weapon is a long belt hook, which is fixed to its left side, and which allowed the pistol to be suspended from the belt. In all my collecting years I have never seen a Tower pistol in such wonderful condition. It was bought many years ago from the collection of George Kellam.

12-inch DRAGOON FLINTLOCK PISTOL

Length: 19 in.
Bore: 0.65 in.

At one stage in my collecting, I had built up a more or less complete collection of flint and percussion Tower pistols.

There was, however, one type absent, namely, the 12-inch flintlock Dragoon, which was the Army counterpart of the 12-inch sea-service pistol. Even several years ago, this could not be acquired for much less than four figures.

One day, I was shown a pistol with a nine-inch barrel, the entire fore-end of the stock being broken off.

The barrel had the normal Tower proof marks, and the lock, which was extensively pitted, revealed no trace whatsoever of the Royal Cypher. The scarcely decipherable signature of Galton, a well-known private maker of military firearms, and the date, 1760, were on the tail.

On the obverse side of the gun was the outline of a serpentine sideplate, but with no inletting whatsoever. All these features, and the butt-cap,

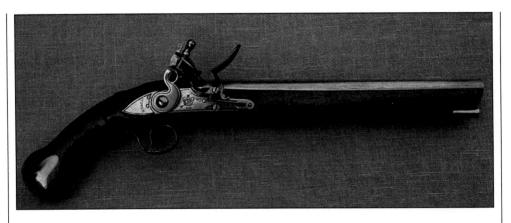

Tower Sea-service pistol

with its long side tangs, were clear evidence that this weapon was a shortened 12-inch Dragoon. Why this had been done is a matter of conjecture. It appeared that the stock had been sanded down at some time in its life, as there was some loss of definition, and the teardrop finials behind the lockplate and sideplate were both absent. Perhaps, too, this explained the apparent absence of inletting for the missing sideplate.

Another interesting feature was that although the lock fitted the lock recess with precision, indicating that the lock was 'right' to the gun, the pan had been ground at a point opposite the vent, in order effectively to lower the pan to this level. Had this modification not been carried out, the lock would have failed to operate the gun, as the pan level would have been too high, and, although most unusual, had been executed in a very professional way. It is my opinion that it was carried out at the time of manufacture of the lock, when, presumably, that batch of locks was found to have unsatisfactory pans, and this modification could have been carried out in order to resolve a difficult problem. However, the Board of Ordnance must have had different sentiments, and the weapon was in all probability sold off after being rejected by them.

It was now my happy task to restore this weapon to its original state. Firstly, it was necessary to add three inches to the barrel, and this was carried out using steel tubing of the appropriate bore. The mount for the barrel pin was silver-soldered to the new section, and the whole barrel was then filed to remove all trace of the weld, and struck up. It was then aged in such a manner as to produce a slightly dull finish.

There were now no signs whatsoever that the

barrel had ever been other than twelve inches in length. The muzzle was lightly filed, and rounded off to produce the appearance of wear that one would expect to find on a weapon which had been in use by the military.

A piece of walnut of matching grain and colour was found, about six inches long, and spliced into the broken stock. This was roughly shaped before glueing, and finally finished off when the glue had set, being smoothed, and sanded down to match the contours of the existing stock. It was then drilled to receive a barrel pin, which was turned in the lathe.

A ramrod pipe was constructed to the correct size and style, using cast brass of a similar colour to the other brasswork on the pistol. This, too, was fixed in position.

One or two minor stock repairs were carried out, always ensuring that the grain in the new wood ran in the same direction as that in the stock.

A ramrod with a brass tip was then constructed in the lathe and the outline of the serpentine sideplate was formed, firstly on paper, then on thin metal, and finally on cast brass. This was a delicate and difficult job as the sideplate is rounded in section and is also contoured in itself. The stock was slightly inletted to receive it, and the sideplate itself was drilled with holes for its two securing sidenails. New sidenails were fabricated, each large enough to accommodate the extra thickness of the sideplate within its width, and the screw heads were slightly distressed in order to be in keeping with the general state of the pistol.

Lastly, the lockplate was filed, then sanded and polished smooth again. The old engraving was identified and deepened so that the markings were once more crisp and clearly outlined.

This was a massive restoration, and it could be

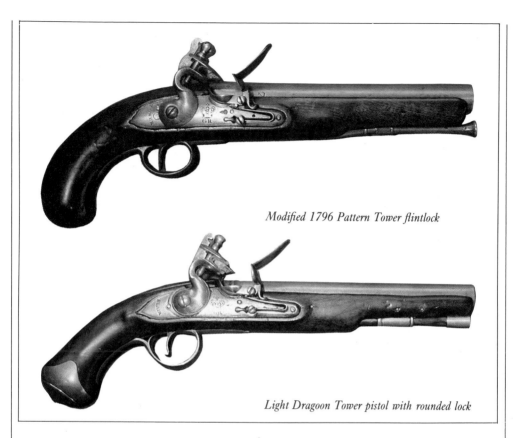

Modified 1796 Pattern Tower flintlock

Light Dragoon Tower pistol with rounded lock

argued that such work is taking restoration too far. However, I am quite firm in my belief that this pistol was designed as a 12-inch Dragoon, and although, perhaps for convenience in carriage, it had been shortened to nine inches, I felt entirely justified in restoring it to the situation for which it was originally intended.

HEAVY DRAGOON FLINTLOCK PISTOL – MODIFIED 1796 PATTERN

Length: 15 in.
Barrel length: 9 in.
Bore: 0.75 in.

This weapon was in excellent condition when I purchased it. All the parts were original, including the metal ramrod, which was held in position by a 'throat-hole' brass ramrod pipe, and the markings were crisp and sharp. At some time it must have been secured to a wall, because the barrel was discoloured in a distinct band near the muzzle. This disfigurement had to be removed, and the barrel was then evenly recoloured.

Such treatment restored the weapon to, more or less, its original state.

The trigger-guard of this gun was engraved '3 D – G' (Third Dragoon Guards).

LIGHT DRAGOON FLINTLOCK PISTOL

Length: 15 in.
Barrel length: 9 in.
Bore: 0.65 in.

This round-locked pistol, which was also in superb condition, had the name 'Blair' engraved across the tail of the lock. There had been a small repair made to the fore-end, but this was perfectly acceptable in that the direction of the grain and the colour of the wood completely blended with the stock. The single ramrod pipe for this pattern of pistol was, however, a replacement, and its bronze hue was not in keeping with the distinctive yellow colour of the antique brass of the butt-cap and trigger-guard.

Using my lathe, I turned a piece of brass of matching colour, and of the correct length and style, polishing the completed piece to remove all traces of the lathe tool, and fitted the pipe into position on the gun.

The overall appearance was then exemplary.

PAGET'S FLINTLOCK PISTOL

Length: 15 in.
Barrel length: 9 in.
Bore: 0.65 in.

This is a much rarer Tower pistol. The lock is quite remarkable, the sharpness of the engraving and the crispness of the action being outstanding. The gun is distinguished from other Tower pistols by its stepped and bolted lock (i.e., safety bolt).

This gun had had a repair to the stock made at some time which was less than perfect. The stock was very dark and had been varnished. Now if there is one thing I cannot bear in an antique gun it is the sight of varnish on the stock.

There is only one way to bring out the natural beauty and grain of wood, and that is the traditional method of application of linseed oil, which, over a period of time, produces a rubbed oil finish which cannot be remotely imitated by varnish.

Varnish masks the grain and colour of a gunstock, whereas oil and polish bring these out. The very presence of thick varnish and stain should alert the wary collector to the possibility of some underlying mischief – possibly an ill-matching repair.

Consequently, my first act on finding a weapon with a varnished stock is to strip this finish off.

When I had stripped this stock down, I discovered that, whilst the repair was perfect in execution, the grain ran at right angles to the grain of the stock! It was to hide this imperfection in technique that the stock had been stained darkly, and hidden further by thick varnish. Why someone who has the considerable skills necessary to repair shattered woodwork should negate what would otherwise be an excellent piece of workmanship by this elementary blunder is totally incomprehensible to me. Undoubtedly it is much easier to splice in any old piece of timber without the necessity of matching grain or type, and I suppose that a sense of satisfaction with one's achievements can be secondary to a desire for quick financial gain. Thus it was necessary to find a piece of straight-grained reddish walnut, which is the usual gunstock material for military weapons. The stock was then repaired for the second time in its life, but this time the result was perfect, and was totally undetectable, even at close range.

This is a good example of how a gun can be saved by correct and skilful restoration.

NEW LAND PATTERN FLINTLOCK PISTOL

Length: 15 in.
Barrel length: 9 in.
Bore: 0.65 in.

This was my very first Tower pistol. Its barrel had a polished finish and showed not the slightest trace of corrosion. Its stock was unblemished and the lock markings were crisply sharp.

This model of Tower pistol had an attached swivel ramrod, without ramrod pipes. New Land Pattern pistols were originally supplied in pairs, at a cost of £2 4s. 2d. per pair.

New Land Pattern Tower flintlock. Note swivel ramrod

Tower Percussion Pistols

COASTGUARD PISTOL

Length: 11in.
Barrel length: 6 in.
Bore: 0.65 in.

When I purchased this pistol at a local auction both the swivel ramrod and the hammer were missing. In addition, the barrel tang was fractured, there was no ramrod pipe and there were several chips in the stock.

The gun was, however, an early example of this type of pistol, as could be seen from an inspection of the lock. Lovell, who was Master of Ordnance at that time, wanted to use up obsolete flintlock parts, and the lock on this pistol was of that type.

The tail of the lockplate was engraved 'Tower', while the Royal Cypher was represented by a solitary crown. Proof marks were post-1813 Birmingham type.

I had a ramrod pipe made and fitted, as well as a swivel ramrod. I then repaired the stock damage. A replacement hammer was ordered from a specialist firm and was then appropriately aged and fitted to the gun.

This type of pistol was used by the Coastguard, and had a sling swivel in the butt as well as a belt hook on the left side of the stock. It had a calibre of 0.56 inches.

This example, however, had no belt hook, and a calibre of 0.65 inches, and was therefore a military pistol. In this form it was issued to police and Land Transport Corps, and to forces in New South Wales and Van Diemen's Land.

ENFIELD PISTOL

Length: 15 in.
Barrel length: 10 in.
Bore: 0.577 in.

This enormous pistol, which was obsolete by the time of its issue, since by then the revolver had proved to be a dependable weapon, has a rifled barrel, a foresight and a three-leaf rearsight. The lockplate is engraved 'Enfield 1856', together with the Royal Cypher. There is a swivel ramrod. Proof marks are those of the Enfield factory, and include an Enfield stamp on the stock. The butt-cap was engraved on its tang, 'E.C.Y.C.' (East Cheshire Yeomanry Cavalry).

Some Enfield pistols could be converted to a carbine by attaching a shoulderstock through a slot in the butt. They used the same ammunition as the Enfield rifle.

The hammer was missing from this gun when I purchased it, but fortunately I was able to obtain an excellent casting, which, after ageing, blended perfectly with the barrel and lock.

Coastguard percussion pistol

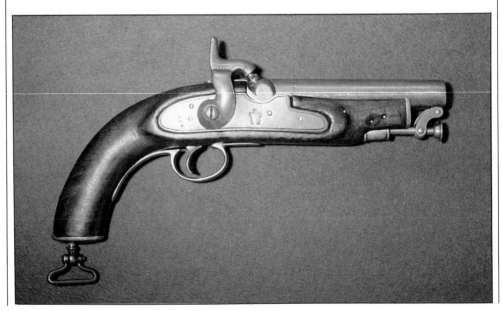

64

Enfield percussion pistol. Note fore- and rearsights, and lanyard ring.

The flat barrel wedge was broken, and I filed a new one from a piece of solid steel and carefully aged this to match the colour of the other steel parts. The stock was then polished with linseed oil to re-create the former glory of this magnificent pistol.

EAST INDIA COMPANY PERCUSSION PISTOL

Length: 14 in.
Barrel length: 8 in.
Bore: 0.65 in.

This weapon is a single-shot percussion pistol with an eight-inch barrel. Its butt-cap incorporates a lanyard ring, in keeping with its function as a cavalry pistol.

Proof marks are of the post-1813 Birmingham type. The lockplate markings are a crown surmounting E.I.G. (East India Government) and Birmingham 1867.

The gun was manufactured in Birmingham for the East India Company, and superficially resembles the Enfield pistol, but is smoothbore and has a shorter barrel. Both weapons have swivel ramrods.

I purchased this weapon from Henry Wrigley.

POLICE PERCUSSION PISTOL

Length: 9½ in.
Barrel length: 4½ in.
Bore: 0.653 in.

This very compact and sturdy Tower pistol has a swivel ramrod and the metal parts have a dull steel finish. The gun is in excellent condition, and the proof marks are clear and unblemished.

The left frame is engraved 'Tower 1848', with the Royal Cypher, a crowned V.R., on the right. Irish registration marks, of Dublin Castle, are engraved on the breech, as well as the late-type Tower proof marks.

This pistol was issued to the Irish Constabulary, and was originally supplied in a leather holster.

I have seen examples of this holster, but have never seen a police percussion pistol in such excellent condition as this one.

Only 500 of these weapons were manufactured.

The Collecting Instinct

How can I convey to my reader the thrill and fascination of collecting? These are intangible sensations, their definition elusive.

For the collector, each day that dawns is one of excitement, a venture into the unknown, since he never knows at what moment he will be fortunate enough to find a new item to grace his collection.

It can happen almost instantaneously – a chance remark by a friend or a colleague at work, a glance into the window of an antique shop during the lunch break, a trip to the local flea-market, and what makes it even more thrilling is that it can happen at any time, and does very often, when least expected.

How can one express in words the quickening pulse when one comes across a new object, the feeling of anticipation when a possible new source is approached – this is the magic world of the collector, and whether one collects stamps or paperweights, bottle openers or objets d'art, the feeling is exactly the same.

All collectors are united in spirit, and have an affinity and rapport with one another.

Why we all have this acquisitive instinct is arguable, and probably beyond the scope of this book.

I have no doubt that the psychologists would tell us that we all have deep-seated feelings of insecurity that lead us to horde our possessions in order to bolster our self-confidence. A more thoughtful and understanding viewpoint is that it represents a desire to prevent change, to maintain the standards of the old world.

On the other hand, perhaps it is merely a wish to preserve things of beauty, in order to prevent them being lost forever.

Whatever the reasons may be, the collector preserves the objects he desires, and displays them to gratify his own self-indulgence, yet all who are privileged to share in his private world are left with a sense of wonderment, which is evident even to the casual observer.

Each piece is presented with a reverence which cannot fail to influence even the most scornful among his audience, who leave the shrine with a mixture of astonishment and admiration, and even, may I suggest, a hint of envy.

Such is the world of the collector.

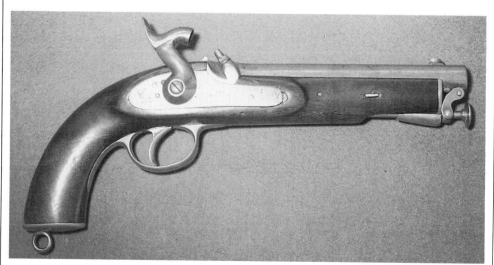

East India Company percussion cavalry pistol

Characters Encountered

I have always regarded Henry Wrigley as the doyen of collectors of antique guns. He was a marvellous character, a man in his sixties when I met him, but who had been collecting all his life. He used to describe himself as a two-time loser, which, in his interpretation, meant that he had been married for the second time – very happily too, I might add.

Henry was, first and foremost, a collector, and he dealt only in order to buy more guns. We recognized in each other the same enthusiasm, and therefore we were in tune with one another.

A week never went by without Henry making a purchase of some kind, and on a Saturday morning in Fred Tomlinson's shop, out would come the latest acquisition for general appraisal. He was a real expert, and capable of the most intricate restoration.

To a certain extent we were rivals, because he and I vied with one another for the weapons which came into Fred's hands. Fred, of course, being well known as a specialist dealer in weapons and scientific instruments, tended to get the bulk of such items in the Stockport area, and it was often a case of first come, first served. I always felt a little 'put-out' when Henry beat me to it, but, on the other hand, he had been collecting for many years before me, and therefore had greater resources on which to draw in terms of 'trade-in' weapons.

Henry was also adept at, and interested in, casing antique guns, and I well remember attending a lecture that he delivered to the Stockport and District Arms Collectors' Society on this subject. Thus, we were both specialists of a kind.

On one occasion, he remarked to me, 'You and I are very alike, you don't mind spending a bit more to get what you want.'

This was absolutely true then, and still is today. After all, the great axiom of the antique trade generally is that an item is worth whatever a collector is prepared to pay for it, and, of course, there may be no limit to the amount a collector is prepared to pay for an item he dearly wants.

I was greatly saddened to hear of his sudden death. To many of us, the world of antique firearms has never been quite the same since.

Another of the great characters of the antique gun business is George Wentworth. He was one of the people fortunate enough to start collecting many years ago, when cased English revolvers could be bought for £4 10s. rather than the five or six hundred pounds one would require today.

George has held me spellbound with his talk of Stan Finlow, who had a shop on Lancashire Hill, and used to sell pistols for '2s. 6d. in that box, 5s. in the other, and any weapons in the glass case 10s.'

An expert on Scottish pistols, George had, up until a few years ago, a most comprehensive collection of these fascinating weapons, which he would from time to time display at Arms Exhibitions. His range of pistols began with the very early weapons with heart-shaped butts, progressing through the scroll-butted variety with silver inlay, and ending with the very elegant mid-18th century ramshorn pistol of classic form.

George has cased duelling pistols, early Queen Anne pistols, Colt revolvers, and all in superb condition.

His knowledge of Colt revolvers is profound, especially early Colts. He often used to bring, for our perusal, some fabulous Colt Dragoon with squareback trigger-guard, or a cased Police revolver with ivory grips. Sometimes it would be a cased pair of duelling pistols, and I well remember a cased set of Gastinne Renette French duellers, in their fitted French-style case with all their accessories, that turned out to be breech loading – what a rarity!

George has the type of antique gun in his collection that makes his fellow collectors drool. His flintlocks are almost invariably early examples, and as such are generally more elegant and desirable than later models.

In my search for antique firearms, I used to visit one area regularly. Time after time, shopowners would say, 'Yes, I had a gun last week, but I sold it to Joe Bloggs,' or, 'Have you tried Joe Bloggs, he has all the antique guns round here?'

After a while, I began to develop something of a complex about this man, and, in the course of time, when I happened to be on holiday in this part of the country, I decided to pay him a visit.

We soon began to get on well together, which is quite usual when collectors share the same interest.

His collection was hanging on the walls of his lounge, and comprised perhaps sixty or so antique guns. What roused my interest most was that no attempt had been made to repair any weapon, or replace parts, so that one weapon might have a hammer missing, another a ramrod, a third minus its frizzen, and so on, and he obviously felt that it was best to leave these weapons as they were.

This illustrates the different views of collectors; there are the two schools of thought, to repair or not to repair, and one acts according to the way one feels.

There was one particular gun, not on display, that I was more than a little interested in. It had a brass barrel and lock, and was in untouched condition. The trigger-guard was intact, but the bottom half of the butt, including the butt-cap, was broken off and missing.

When I showed an interest in buying this gun, however, and indeed made him a substantial offer (having incidentally already repaired it in my mind's eye) I could see that his attitude had completely changed, and that there was no way that he would be persuaded to sell it to me, even although he himself had had no interest in it before.

I have witnessed this phenomenon time and time again, and, indeed, have acted in precisely the same manner myself. If another collector becomes interested in something that you yourself attach no importance to, you begin to ask yourself, 'Why is he so interested? I must be missing something, or he wouldn't be so keen.'

My fellow collector must have felt, 'If he thinks he can repair the gun, then obviously it can be done, and maybe some time I will find someone who can do it.'

We all witness the same thing at flea-markets. If someone standing next to us picks up an object and starts to examine it closely, our own interest is aroused, and we hope and pray that he will put the item down so that we can purchase it. Nevertheless I was very disappointed.

Gun Paradise

I pushed open the door of the little room with trembling hand, and stepped into Paradise itself. Sworn to secrecy by the character who had brought me, in deference to his wishes I make no mention of his name in this account.

The walls on both sides of the room were literally covered in antique pistols, so that there was no space to accommodate a single extra gun. I tried to count the weapons that were on display, but soon gave up the attempt. There were twenty-odd pairs of Queen Anne pistols, pairs of flintlock pistols of every description, military pistols, percussion pistols – the list and numbers of guns seem endless. Hanging over a chair was a pair of holsters, each containing a Colt Navy revolver. On the floor, cases of pistols were piled high – a pair of Wogdon duelling pistols, a cased pair of Colt Navy revolvers with all their accessories. Even now, I sometimes wonder if it really happened, that any collector could possibly accumulate so much.

'You must come back any time,' he said. But I never did, preferring instead to preserve the unreal and dreamlike quality of the experience in my memory.

Peter and Wendy Dyson complete my catalogue of characters of the antique gun trade.

A gunsmith specializing in antique weapons, Peter has built up a thriving business in Yorkshire. For many years he has produced large quantities of high-quality reproduction accessories, each one accurately copied from an original item, and I have happy memories of rummaging in an enormous chest at his workshop, crammed with original accessories of every description. His wife, Wendy, who has given me a number of useful tips, including the secret of ageing ivory, collects powder flasks. She is an expert in the casing of antique weapons, and has been a great help to me in this respect.

Queen Anne Flintlock Coach Pistol by Richards

RICHARDS, Thomas (1740–1780)
Shop in London. Made cannon-
barrelled flintlock pocket pistols and
Queen Anne flintlock coach pistols. Also
flintlock holster pistols under Royal
Government contract.

Length: 12 in.	
Barrel length: 5 in.	
Bore: 0.62 in.	

When I acquired this flintlock pistol by Thomas Richards at an Arms Fair, the overall finish was of a brown appearance, due to the effects of rusting and polishing over several years.

The gun was, in the terminology of the antique gun business, a 'sleeper', which means that it had never had any work of any kind done to it, and was being presented for sale in the condition in which it had first come to light.

All parts were present and original. The gun itself had a cannon barrel of the 'screw-off' variety, a walnut stock with a silver grotesque mask butt-cap, a shield-shaped silver escutcheon and a silver serpentine sideplate.

There is a safety catch which operates by sliding forward the trigger-guard, so locking the tumbler as well as slotting into the back of the trigger. As the normal finish accepted by collectors for pistols of this type is of bright polished steel, I attempted to remove the brown appearance of the metal parts but, when I did so, I was appalled by the degree of pitting uncovered by the removal of this deposit. I could see that the restoration of the pistol would take a considerable amount of time.

Working painstakingly on each part, I gradually removed all traces of pitting, using finer and finer grades of wet and dry sandpaper, finally polishing with wire wool. The parts were then lightly dulled to produce the desired effect of age on the bright metal, and, when completed, the pistol was restored to its former elegance.

The restoration took many weeks of work, but the end result is a gun of beautiful lines and classic form, preserved for posterity.

There is an interesting story concerning screw barrel pistols, which I think is worth repeating.

During the English Civil War of the 17th century, the Royalist Army was passing through Stafford. When they reached St Mary's Church, Prince Rupert, who was armed with a pair of these pistols, took aim at the cock on the weathervane of the church steeple and fired, hitting the target, whereupon King Charles I commented that it had been a lucky shot.

Prince Rupert then drew the second pistol from his saddle holster, aimed, and fired again at the weathervane, and again his shot found the target.

Such legends are the bread and butter on which the antique gun collector thrives.

Barrel unscrewed for loading

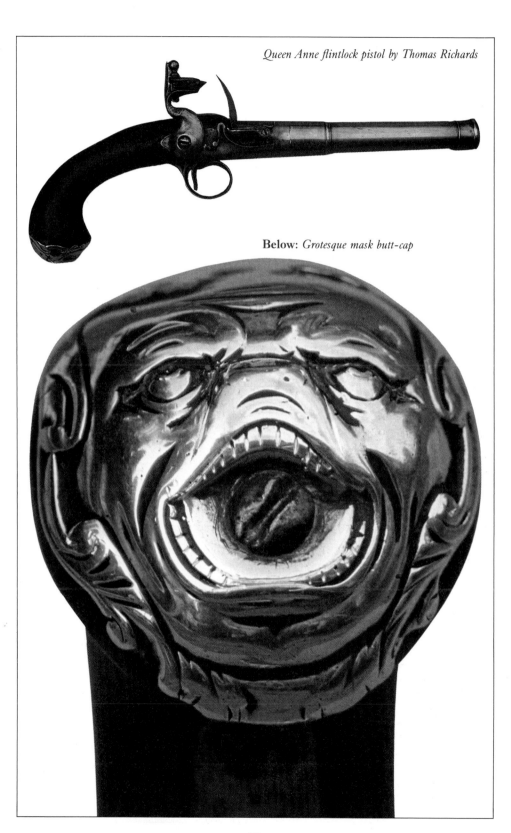

Queen Anne flintlock pistol by Thomas Richards

Below: *Grotesque mask butt-cap*

Transition Revolver by Joseph Harkom

HARKOM, Joseph (*c.* 1850)
Shop in Edinburgh, Scotland. Made
percussion pepperboxes and transition
revolvers. Also made cased percussion
holster pistols.

I have only seen two examples of this Scottish gunsmith's work, and one was a transition revolver in my own collection.

This type of revolver was, in effect, a transition between the pepperbox and the true revolver, and represents a natural development from the pepperbox, which it resembles, with the solid barrel block being replaced by a single barrel, and with a revolving five-chambered cylinder. Like the pepperbox, the transition revolver has a bar hammer, and the nipples are arranged coaxially.

The weapon had 100 per cent of its original blueing, with a butt trap at the base to hold percussion caps. The cylinder had retained all of its case hardening, and I can say, in all honesty, that I have never seen a revolver which has been as well preserved as this one.

Normally, for a weapon to be in this state of preservation, it has to be kept in a case, and this, in fact, is what had happened. When the gun was acquired, it was indeed in its original fitted case, although with all of its accessories missing. The trade label of Harkom was stuck inside the upper lid. However, the owner would not part with the case at any price, as he had another use for it, and nothing would induce him to change his mind.

I obviously had to accept this, but decided that I should make an attempt to case the weapon.

I had never done this before, but was very keen to try. As I have explained elsewhere in this book, it would be pointless to use new cloth, so I chose to use old velvet material of a purplish hue, which I had purchased a long time previously with this aim in mind.

When I bought the Harkom revolver, I purchased at the same time a fine mahogany instrument box with exactly the same dimensions as the gun. This box had to be altered, since English gunboxes invariably have what are known as 'break-back' hinges, which keep the lid in the vertical position when opened.

I managed to obtain a suitable pair of hinges from an old box at a local flea-market, and duly fitted them.

The key plate was missing, so a piece of old brass had to be found, filed into shape, the keyhole filed into it, and the plate carefully glued into position in the case.

Next, the side pieces, which fit around the perimeter of the base, were constructed from old mahogany and mitred into place. These pieces were then angled where they obtruded above the bottom of the case, in order to allow the lid to close in position, and the material was cut to the correct size and glued to the base and lid of the box.

The gun was then laid down in the box so that a decision could be made regarding the situation and number of the various compartments. Gradually a plan emerged, and thin pieces of softwood were obtained, cut to size, sanded down to form a triangular section, and mitred where necessary. These were then carefully covered with velvet and glued into position in the case.

Afterwards, a bullet mould of suitable size was found and purchased, lead balls were cast and aged and a flask of the appropriate size was taken from my collection, as well as a tin of percussion caps.

In the course of time a turnscrew, a nipple key and a cleaning rod were added to the case.

I think that for a first casing this was a very reasonable job, and was not detected when the gun was disposed of.

I feel strongly that, where at all possible, only original accessories should be used when casing weapons. Reproductions, if used, should be replaced with originals at the earliest opportunity.

Coincidentally, in the only other cased Harkom revolver I have seen, the case lining was of purple velvet.

Colt Army Revolver, 1860

Length: 14 in.
Barrel length: 8 in.
Bore: 0.44 in.

I have owned two of these guns; the first was in excellent condition, although the serial number on the cylinder did not match that on the rest of the gun.

At some time it must have been fired with too great a charge of gunpowder, because a distinct bulge was present in the first inch of the eight-inch barrel. I have noted this on several other Colt Army revolvers.

I eventually replaced this gun with the one now in my collection. This has all matching serial numbers, and is also in excellent condition, with some original blueing in evidence around the base of the hammer and creeping lever ramrod. All of the colour hardening of the frame is still present. The cylinder is six-shot.

The butt is stamped at the base with a Government Inspector's mark. This, together with the serial number, indicates that the gun was made, and in all probability used, during the American Civil War, 1861–1865.

The revolver is in its original leather Army flap holster, made to be worn on the right for the draw with the right hand, awkward as this may seem.

The original owner must have customized the weapon because the walnut stock has contemporary chequering. This could have been carried out at the end of the Civil War, but I believe was probably done shortly after issue.

Photograph of Jesse James as a young man. Note his three Colt Army revolvers! Library of Congress, Washington

The muzzle of the gun shows slight wear from repeated drawing and replacing of the gun in its holster.

The engraving consists of the single line New York address, 'Address Col. Saml. Colt, New York, U.S. America'.

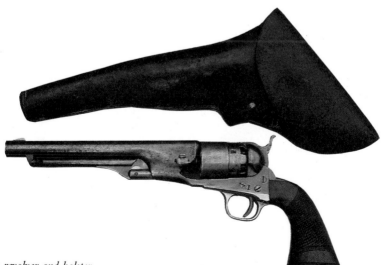

Colt Army revolver and holster

77

Cased Percussion Revolver
by Osborne

OSBORNE, Charles (1858–1900)
Shops in London and Birmingham.
Made double-barrel percussion pistols,
percussion pepperboxes, and revolvers of
Webley Bentley type.

This weapon is of the Webley Bentley type, having a spring safety on the left side of the frame, which engages on the hammer when required.

It is five-shot, with a nine-grooved, rifled barrel, and has a bright overall finish. I am certain that this was its original finish.

The mahogany case is in magnificent condition and, although there is no trade label in the lid, the gun is most certainly, as one can see from the pressure points, original to the case, although when I bought the weapon, some insignificant repairs to the case were necessary.

Apart from the gun, the only other object in the case was the cleaning rod, whose cap was jammed on, but this item was otherwise in pristine condition. After soaking in release oil for several days, it opened to reveal a sharp and bright tapered screw, and I believe I was the first person to look on this screw since the cleaning rod left the workshop of Charles Osborne.

I am of the opinion that the weapon had been recently fired, because the five nipples, which appeared to be in new condition on the outside, had all been broken, probably by the hammer of the gun falling onto them, because where the nipples had fractured the crystallization of the metal due to age was all too apparent. This theory presupposes that not long before I purchased the weapon, accessories for loading and firing must have been in the case.

However, I now had to set about finding appropriate accessories to complete the outfit. The condition of the weapon itself made it essential that such accessories should be in a similar state of preservation.

I first acquired a revolver mould of the correct size – 54-bore – from a Weller and Dufty sale. Next, a revolver flask from my collection was found. This was a rare type in pristine condition, with an embossed revolver on one side and with all its original finish. A bone nipple box, into which I placed the original nipples, and which I had discovered in a junk shop in Ayr, was inserted into its compartment. Over the next few months I added a rare and original Joyce embossed cap tin, a nipple key, turnscrew and oil bottle. The broken nipples were then replaced.

This was a superb example of an English cased revolver, and attracted a great deal of attention from arms dealers when it was in my possession.

Cased percussion revolver by Charles Osborne

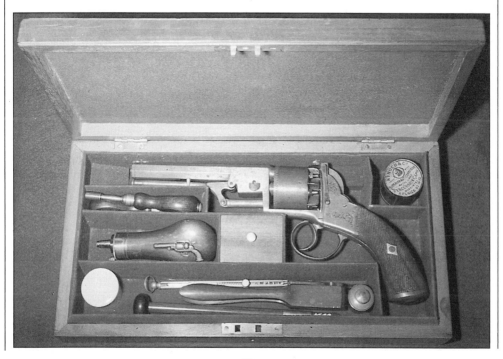

Nest Egg

In Glasgow there was, and maybe even still is, an antique shop called Muirhead Moffat. I ventured into this rather prestigious establishment, in the early days of my collecting, asking the eternal question, 'Have you got any old guns?'

This enquiry, whilst seeming to be innocent enough at first, was, in fact, a carefully constructed subterfuge, since it had a twofold effect.

Firstly, the question presupposes that if the answer to the enquiry is in the affirmative, then by definition the old gun referred to could not be worth very much anyway, and, secondly, the fact that the questioner has referred to antique weapons in such a non-technical way causes the hearer to presume that the questioner cannot be a collector and therefore would not be prepared to pay very much to obtain the old gun.

In response to my enquiry, the assistant proceeded to a cupboard below an old oak dresser, and brought out several antique guns for my perusal.

I can recall each perfectly, to this day.

The first was a double-barrelled percussion overcoat pistol, with a spring bayonet, by John Blisset of Liverpool. The weapon had a bright overall appearance and was in pristine condition.

Next was a pair of flintlock muff pistols by Sharpe. These pistols were again crisp and sharp in every detail, and, like the Blisset pistol, had no replacement parts whatsoever.

The third item was a pair of percussion belt pistols by McDermott of Ireland, in their original green baize-lined fitted mahogany case. They were fullstocked, with the typical Irish flared butts, and swivel ramrods. They had originally been flintlocks, and had been converted to percussion by the drum and nipple method. This was commonly done by owners who valued their pistols sufficiently to make the conversion rather than purchase new weapons.

The guns had their entire original finish, and their case was crammed with accessories for cleaning and loading the weapons, as well as a trade label in the upper lid.

I was very keen to purchase these Irish guns, but at that time collectors were less than happy about conversions, preferring to collect either flintlock or percussion weapons but not something lying between the two, and this is the reason I declined to take them.

Lastly, there was a magnificent pair of double-barrelled flintlock holster pistols with ten-inch barrels by Lacy, as crisp as the other guns and surpassing any I have seen of that type since.

I came out of Muirhead Moffat's without having made a single purchase, since, as I have said, this was early in my collecting life, and each piece was quite a considerable amount of money, even in those far-off days.

The effect of inflation, combined with the ever increasing demand for high-quality guns, is such that had I bought this entire small collection of antique firearms it would have provided a very comfortable nest egg in retirement.

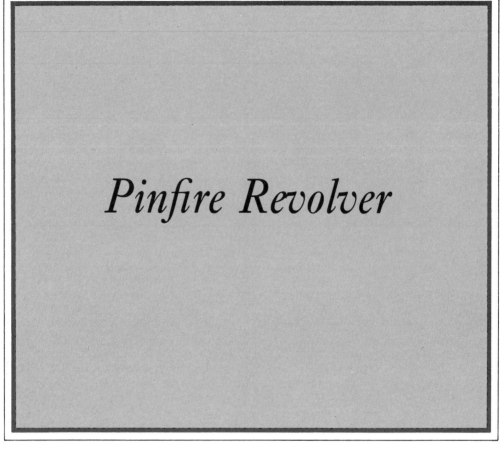

Pinfire Revolver

This weapon was given to me by an old friend, along with a plain Dixon gun flask, which had several parts missing.

Over a period of time I managed to repair the flask's patent top, using an original cut-off and thumbpiece and even an original spring.

This revolver was used with cartridges that had a tiny pin at the rear end, which, when struck by the hammer, detonated the percussion cap inside.

The gun was Belgian-made, with Liège proof marks and, as in all such weapons, had a folding trigger without any guard and the grips were beautifully made of light wood, possibly ash, and were finally chequered. The trigger spring is almost invariably absent or fractured in these guns.

This particular example had been entirely silver-plated, but this had worn off in most places. It was, however, a good representative piece of its type.

Due, however, to a controversy in these days as to whether or not this type of gun required a Firearms Certificate – this depended on which police authority was approached on the subject – I decided to part with the gun, although nowadays there is no restriction, to the best of my knowledge, on pinfire weapons, provided these are kept for antique purposes only.

Turkish Pistol

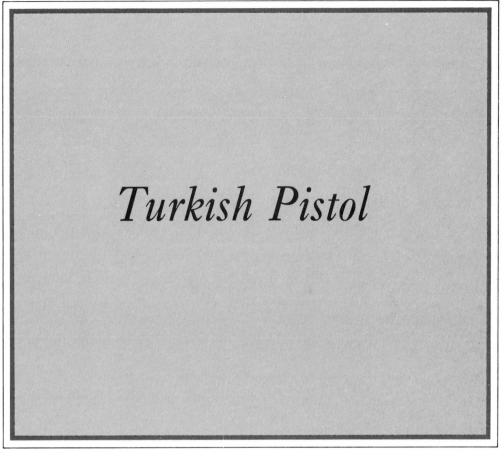

This weapon is a flintlock holster pistol with silver mounts that was found at an auction in Macclesfield. It is of the usual type, having a flared butt and Damascus barrel.

The lockplate and cock are of flat form, the lockplate itself engraved 'Mortimer' in Roman lettering. A foresight is fitted to the barrel, and below is a false ramrod, the true ramrod being suspended from a waist belt when the weapon was in use, as was the custom in pistols of this type. All the furniture, including the fore-end, butt-cap, sideplate and trigger-guard are of silver, the butt-cap having long side tangs.

A red cord was wrapped around the butt several times, its tasselled ends hanging down below the butt, when I acquired the weapon. I had never seen this arrangement before, but have subsequently discovered that this feature was not uncommonly found in quality Turkish pistols.

The metalwork of the weapon was extremely rusty but unpitted; it was necessary to remove this rust by simmering in caustic soda solution. This gave a dull overall finish which then required to be burnished, using fine-grade wet and dry sandpaper and steel wool. There was also a split in the stock which necessitated repair. This was caused by the mainspring jumping free from the lock and creating pressure on the thin wood below the lock, causing it to fracture. I have found this frequently on antique guns. It is often caused by careless removal of the lock, and can be prevented quite simply by always engaging the half cock bent, before removal.

The presence of the name of an English gunsmith on the lockplate indicates that this weapon was made in England for the Eastern market and is the only one I have ever purchased which I never intended to keep, but simply to repair and sell again.

I made a humble profit, but some months later I saw the weapon again at an Arms Fair, recognizing my own work on the stock, and was astonished to find that it had increased in value to five times its original purchase price.

Adams Revolver

ADAMS, Robert and John (1851–
1892)
Patented a percussion revolver in 1851.
These were made by Deane, Adams and
Deane, of 30 King William St., London.
It was made in three calibres, 0.50 inch,
0.44 inch and 0.32 inch. Later
purchased the Beaumont Patent. Both
patents taken over by the London
Armoury Company.

This weapon was cased in an English oak case with the label of Deane, Adams and Deane stuck inside the lid together with the label of the retailer, a dealer in Devonport. The case was lined with green baize.

The gun itself was an improved 1854 patent Adams revolver, with the Adams rammer, which folded down the left side of the weapon, locating into a slot in the chequered stock.

Adams's original patent was for a double-action revolver, unlike the Colt which had to be cocked each time before firing. The improved version allowed the weapon to be fired either single or double action, and was improved still further two years later with the adoption of Captain Beaumont's patent.

The barrel was rifled and the cylinder five-shot.

The gun shone in its box like a blue jewel, having 100 per cent of its original kingfisher blueing, the accessories comprising mould, cap tin, turnscrew, ball and powder flask. The mould cast a 'tailed' ball for use with a special cartridge known as a 'dustbin cartridge', and could be 'thumb-seated' or loaded with the rammer.

The cleaning rod was not original to the case, and I discarded it, turning one from ebony in the lathe and tipping it with an original worm and cap, which had retained its tarnished appearance and so lent authenticity to the piece.

Some time ago, a panic developed among collectors that antique revolvers would be put 'on ticket', that is to say that they would require a Firearms Certificate, and for this reason, at that time, I reluctantly decided to part with several such revolvers in my collection, including the Adams.

Cased Adams percussion revolver with accessories. This model is the 1854 Improved Frame

Double-Barrelled
Percussion Pistol

This weapon, which dates from about 1840, was purchased from the collection of Henry Wrigley, and although unnamed was nevertheless of high quality.

The locks were of the type known as sidehammer boxlock and had patent nipple blocks which incorporated a screw which was removable in order to facilitate cleaning. The hammers were in the form of engraved dolphins. The butt was finely chequered, terminating in a flat base, with a silver ring around its circumference, and a swivel ramrod was fitted below the barrel block. The barrels were of the 'side by side' variety and were bored out of a single block. Scroll engraving was present on either side of the frame, together with a sunburst on the trigger-guard. Proof marks were of post-1813 Birmingham type, stamped on both barrel and frame. The pistol had an overall brown appearance, due to the effects of age on the original finish.

The gun was a beautiful example of the work of the gunsmith, whose hand, unfortunately, is unknown, although I think that this omission does nothing to reduce the aesthetic or monetary value of the gun. Presumably, as a provincial gunsmith, the maker felt that the addition of his name would be of no assistance in the future sale of the weapon, but the omission is, nonetheless, surprising.

Double-barrelled percussion pistol, with tin of percussion caps by Joyce

Brown Bess

Length: 4 ft. 7 in.
Barrel length: 3 ft. 3 in.
Bore: 0.75 in.

This flintlock smoothbore musket has a 39-inch barrel, and is full stocked to the muzzle.

The lock is engraved 'Tower', with the Royal Cypher and armourer's mark. All furniture is of brass, and the stock of dark walnut. The ramrod is original, as evidenced by the Tower markings engraved upon it and the breech is stamped with Tower proof marks. The gun itself is original in all respects, having no replacement parts.

The 39-inch India Pattern Brown Bess was thought to be inferior to the 42-inch and 46-inch models, but in my opinion this particular weapon was of outstanding quality.

When I removed the barrel pins I discovered that the metal underneath, where protected by the stock, retained its original browning. The name, 'Brown Bess', is thought to derive from an affectionate reference to this barrel finish.

The British soldier had to achieve a rate of fire of four shots per minute with this weapon as the aim was to lay down a field of fire through which the enemy could not pass, as is done today with modern automatic weapons.

The principle was that it did not matter if you hit the man you were aiming at so long as you hit the man next to him, and this was achieved by firing in rows, the first row kneeling and firing, the second row preparing to fire and the third reloading. When you had fired, you fell in to the rear to reload.

The Brown Bess was to remain the principal arm of the British soldier from 1720 until 1845.

Enfield 2-Band Carbine

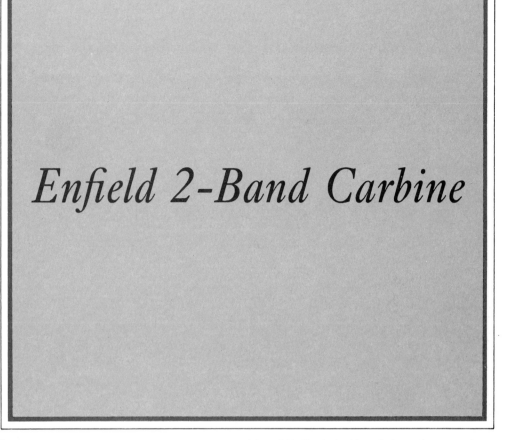

Length: 3 ft. 10 in.
Barrel length: 2 ft. 6 in.
Bore: 0.733 in.

This weapon is full stocked in walnut, with a brass buttplate. The stock is stamped with Enfield markings and is in excellent condition. There is a steel ramrod of the correct pattern, and a sling is fitted between the swivels.

The lockplate is engraved 'Enfield' in Roman lettering, together with the Royal Cypher. Enfield proof marks were engraved on the breech. The weapon had been converted to a breechloader by means of a Snider breechblock.

The metalwork was in dreadful condition when I purchased it – a policeman was in the shop at the time, and made a joke about the 'old gun', but at that time a Snider was definitely not permitted to be sold 'off ticket', although this no longer applies – the barrel was badly pitted, there was no ramrod, and the barrel band nearest the muzzle was missing.

There was nothing to be lost by going 'the whole hog' on this weapon. I filed off all the pitting and struck the barrels up bright. I then fully restored the Snider action.

Managing to obtain an original Enfield ramrod, I cut this down to the correct size, making a screw thread at the base to fit the jags of the Enfield tool.

I then acquired an original barrel band and fitted it to the gun, along with an original sling, which I obtained at the same time.

Lastly, I obtained a nipple protector on its chain, which was fitted over the firing pin.

The barrel was then subjected to a mild dulling of the brightened finish, and the overall result was a weapon which had been completely restored to its original state.

Lancaster Rifle

Length: 4 ft.
Barrel length: 2 ft. 8 in.
Bore: 0.577 in.

The Lancaster oval-bored rifle is a very rare item, and I purchased this example in Ashton-under-Lyne for a few pounds. This type of bore was, in effect, a form of rifling, which was produced in response to a search by Ordnance for a really effective rifle, the various gunsmiths submitting their own designs. This was an experimental design and was not officially adopted.

The stock and barrel had been covered in thick varnish, and this had to be removed before polishing. The barrel was unpitted, and presented a blackened appearance. The point of a pin revealed delicate engraving across the breech – 'C. Lancaster', in Roman lettering. This had been totally obscured by dirt and varnish. Tower markings, and the Royal Cypher, on the lockplate were crisp and clear, and the original metal ramrod also exhibited Tower markings.

The weapon was in virtually new condition after cleaning, yet before the varnish was removed had looked quite unremarkable, and several gun collectors, who had seen the carbine before restoration, had not only been unimpressed by the gun but had completely failed to recognize it for what it was.

Although no longer in my possession, I am proud to have brought this weapon back to its original state.

Antique Dealers

On one occasion, my standard opening gambit rebounded in my face.

I was in the village of Doune, in Stirlingshire, and to my delight noticed an antique shop in the main steet which was actually open.

I went in and found the proprietor engaged in conversation with another dealer.

'Have you any old guns?' I said.

'No, I haven't,' replied the proprietor, and, turning to his colleague, said, 'What does he expect to find here, Doune pistols?' and both men fell about laughing.

Even I could see the funny side.

On another occasion, I walked into an antique shop in the heart of Cheshire.

In response to my enquiry, the proprietor produced a brown paper parcel containing a pocket percussion pistol of poor quality.

She told me the price, but when I examined it, I noted that the gun had been restored and that the trigger-guard was a modern and poorly fitted and constructed replacement.

When I declined to make the purchase, she demanded to know the reason, and when I told her, she began to shout and hurl abuse at me in a most unladylike fashion. I was very glad to gain the comparative safety of the pavement outside.

I remember once going into an antique shop in Stockport and asking to see an old pistol in a window display. Receiving permission to do so, I lifted the gun, but its heavy iron barrel caught the arm of a small porcelain figure, shattering its cuff into fragments.

Hanging in the shop was the standard, but legally indefensible, stanza:

> 'Lovely to look at,
> A joy to behold,
> But if you break it,
> Consider it sold.'

She insisted that I remain in the shop until her husband returned, but as I did not feel constrained to do so, and had grave doubts in any case about the alleged value of the item, I beat a hasty retreat, thrusting some money into her hand, which I felt would be adequate to cover the cost of the repair. The gun itself was a Turkish flintlock, but was only a reproduction.

I was walking past an antique shop in a beautiful village in Dorset when I saw a flintlock fowling piece by Gatehouse of Southampton hanging in the window.

I entered the shop and asked to see the gun. It was in pristine condition, with all the original browning on the barrel. The maker's name was engraved in an oval silver poinçon on the lock-plate, while 'Southampton' was engraved in a similar poinçon on the breech.

The proprietor looked at me and said, 'Are you familiar with the work of Gatehouse?'

Such gratuitous pomposity invariably arouses a proportionate degree of animosity on my part. I doubt if any collector in the country at that time had even heard of this provincial gunsmith, but nevertheless the piece was certainly of very fine quality and workmanship.

The asking price was £150, and today would be worth ten times this figure.

Perhaps if the proprietor had not made his patronizing remark, this weapon would now form part of my collection.

Antique shops, in general, are not ideal finding places for antique firearms at the present time.

Due to widespread dissemination of information about such specialist items as antique weapons, through saleroom catalogues, the publication of antiques price guides and television programmes like the *Antiques Road Show*, any dealer who has a weapon in his shop believes it to be exactly the same as the one illustrated or described, and therefore asks exactly the same amount as this hypothetical weapon, which he has never handled, and has no way of knowing how it might differ from the one in his possession. Invariably, there is the world of difference between the two, and the collector has to leave the piece, knowing that the price is enormously and unjustifiably inflated.

Cased Percussion Pistols by Lewis & Co.

LEWIS and Co. (1840–1860)
Shop in London. Made cased percussion
pocket pistols with loading accessories.

One day, while shopping in Manchester, I came across an original mahogany gunbox which I purchased for a few pounds. I subsequently searched for some months for a suitable pair of pistols in order to make up a cased set, and eventually found a pair of percussion pocket pistols with folding triggers.

These had no original finish whatsoever, but otherwise were one of the crispest pair of pistols I have ever seen.

Years before, I had acquired a red velvet cloth, used for spreading over a bridge table, which was worn and slightly marked, and so was ideal for lining a gunbox.

In the normal manner, I studied as many photographs as possible of cased sets of pocket pistols, searching hundreds of catalogues and every gun book in my possession, and at last decided on a particular format to suit these weapons.

I chose, from my collection, a beautiful flask in perfect condition, which was in keeping with the condition of the weapons themselves, purchased a bullet mould of the correct size and, of course, cast several lead balls.

A more difficult acquisition would be a barrel key, so I decided to make my own, which I managed to do without much difficulty. This was then suitably aged, and added to the set.

Next, a tin of percussion caps was found from my collection, together with a nipple key and a lignum vitae nipple box.

An old key was found which fitted the case lock.

A plan of the various compartments was then drawn up and, using softwood, partitions of the correct size were cut, sandpapered to form an inverted V shape, and finally mitred into position. They were then carefully covered in velvet and glued down to the newly lined base. The lid was padded with flock and the worn red velvet fitted into position over it.

When completed, the appearance of the set justified the many hours that had been spent in its creation. In my own estimation, it was indistinguishable from an original cased set.

Long after I had parted with it, I was at an arms fair and saw the guns for sale on a dealer's stand. I could not help showing a great interest in the weapons and, after a long time, the dealer, who I knew well, said, 'Don't tell me it's one of yours.' I replied, 'There is only one way to tell whether a cased set is original or not, because in an original cased outfit the weapons are not interchangeable in their position in the box.' So saying, I picked up the guns and tried to reverse their positions.

The pistols would not fit.

'This,' I said, 'is *definitely* an original cased set,' tongue firmly in cheek.

Brass-Barrelled Flintlock Overcoat Pistol by Nicholson

NICHOLSON, E. D. (1760–1808)
Shop in Cornhill, London. Made
flintlock pocket pistols and officers'
flintlock holster pistols. Also made cased
duelling pistols.

Length: 8¾ in.
Barrel length: 3 in.
Bore: 0.5 in.

I purchased this pistol from an antique shop in Chester.

Brass-barrelled pistols have always been attractive to collectors of antique firearms, and were well sought after when made initially, since, apart from their aesthetic appeal, the brass barrels and mounts were resistant to rust. This latter characteristic made such weapons particularly desirable at sea.

The mechanism of this pistol was boxlock with centre-swung hammer. The slabsided walnut butt was inlet with a silver escutcheon. The frame, trigger-guard and barrel were all of brass, and the barrel itself of cannon barrel form. Engraving on this weapon was very restrained, consisting of a floral pattern on the trigger-guard and the maker's name, as well as the word 'London', engraved in cartouches on opposite sides of the frame, in Roman lettering. Proof marks were of post-1702 London type. A special feature of this weapon was the sliding safety on the top strap.

In all respects, this was a very neat and attractive flintlock pistol, having no replacement parts of any kind.

Percussion Officer's Pistol by Smith

> **SMITH, Charles T.** (1825–1850)
> Shop in London. Made double-barrel percussion pistols and cased percussion officers' pistols and duelling pistols.

Length: 14½ in.
Barrel length: 8 in.
Bore: 0.65 in.

This weapon was acquired on the same day as the brass-barrelled flintlock pistol.

The lockplate and hammer were of flat section. The gun was fullstocked in walnut, which was hockey-stick shaped in outline, having chequering of good quality. A swivel, sometimes known as a 'captive' ramrod, was fitted below the octagonal barrel. Engraving consisted of the maker's name 'Smith', on the lockplate, with 'London' on the breech, both in Roman lettering, with some scroll engraving on the lockplate and breast of the hammer. Proof marks were of post-1702 London type.

The gun was original in all respects, having no replacement parts, but unfortunately the twist barrels had been blued in recent times, and as such a finish would never have been used on a twist barrel, as blueing does not show this up, this finish was removed, and the barrel 'struck up' and rebrowned.

The method of construction of gun barrels is of some interest here. A quantity of old iron horseshoe nails, often imported from the Continent, was mixed with a varying amount of steel and the whole melted down and formed into long bars of narrow, square section. These were then twisted along their length and hammered on an anvil to a flat strip. This strip was then wound round a mandril whilst red hot and hammered to seal the joints.

Another method consisted of using alternate iron and steel bars and forming the primitive barrel in the same way. Different directions of twist produced the appearance, attractive to many customers, known as Damascus barrels. The crude barrel was then roughly bored out and filed, and finally both the interior and exterior of the barrel were smoothed out and polished.

Percussion Overcoat Pistol with Spring Bayonet by Moore

> **MOORE, Charles** (1780–1835)
> Shop at 77 St James St., London.
> Made officers' flintlock holster pistols
> with spring bayonets. Also made
> percussion duelling pistols and
> percussion pocket pistols with spring
> bayonet.

Length: 8¾ in.
Barrel length: 3 in.
Bore: 0. 45 in.

Charles Moore was a very well known and respected gunsmith in London. This example of his work was a simple percussion boxlock pistol with a centre-swung hammer.

The stock was of walnut, which was bagshaped and finely chequered. An oval silver escutcheon was fitted. The barrel was quite plain and rounded in section. The bore of the weapon, at the muzzle end, was star-shaped, in order to receive the special tapered-shank key which unscrewed the barrel for loading. The maker's name was engraved on one side of the frame and, on the other, 'London', in Roman lettering, amidst scrolling foliage. A sunburst was engraved on the trigger-guard.

Post-1813 Birmingham proof marks were impressed on the barrel and frame. A special feature of this pistol was the triangular section steel bayonet, which was folded beneath the barrel, and which sprang fowards when the trigger-guard was pulled back. It was the presence of this bayonet which led me to purchase this otherwise rather unattractive piece in the first place.

It has been said that such a weapon could be used as a dagger, after the gun had been fired, but I have recently seen a new and quite acceptable theory, that probably it was used as a dagger in the first place, presumably as a deterrent, but, if required, the gun could then be fired. Either theory could find acceptance.

Percussion Overcoat Pistol by Page

> **PAGE, Thomas** (1766–1776)
> Shop in Norwich, Norfolk. Made
> cannon barrel boxlock flintlock pocket
> pistols and flintlock holster pistols.

Length: 9 in.
Barrel length: 3½ in.
Bore: 0.45 in.

This is an attractive weapon, having a cannon barrel and a slabsided stock of polished ebony, which is entirely inlaid with silver wiring in scroll form.

The mechanism is boxlock, with centre-swung hammer of dolphin shape. The barrel is of the 'turn-off' variety. Engraving consists of 'T. Page', and 'Norwich', respectively, engraved in Roman lettering on either side of the frame, amidst scrolling foliage. Proof marks are early London in type.

From the general appearance of this pistol, it could be deduced that it had formerly been a flintlock, which had been converted to percussion by substituting a percussion hammer for the cock, removing the frizzen and boss, filling the recess for the frizzen spring and tapping the vent in order to fit a nipple.

Such conversions are a trifle ugly and, although easily carried out, are not sought after by collectors, since the percussion hammer and nipple look somewhat incongruous against the other features of a pistol which was obviously designed as a flintlock.

Officer's Flintlock Holster Pistol by Simmonds

> **SIMMONDS, Joseph** (1802–1845)
> Shop in Birmingham. Made flintlock
> fowling pieces and flintlock officers'
> holster pistols.

Length: 15 in.
Barrel length: 9 in.
Bore: 0. 75 in.

This flintlock holster pistol was of very large bore and dimensions. The lockplate and cock were of flat section. The stock was of hockey-stick shape, fullstocked to the muzzle, with fine chequering of the butt. There was no butt-cap, but an oval silver escutcheon was inlet behind the barrel tang. A swivel ramrod was fitted below the barrel.

The barrel itself was of round section, with a beautiful dark patina that clearly showed the twist pattern of its construction. The maker's name, Simmonds, was engraved in Roman lettering on the lockplate. Proof marks were of post-1813 Birmingham type.

A special feature of the weapon was the roller bearing fitted to the toe of the frizzen. Sometimes this bearing was fitted instead to the toe of the frizzen spring and assisted in the smooth operation of the lock. This pistol was in superb condition, the stock retaining its original lacquering in its entirety.

It must have belonged originally to an officer who chose to provide his own weapon rather than accept the Modified 1796 Pattern, to which it bears some resemblance, having exactly the same dimensions, bore and length of barrel.

When I purchased this gun it had no ramrod, and I had one made and coloured it to match the dark appearance of the barrel.

Flintlock Pocket Pistol by Whitney

WHITNEY, Patrick (1735–1795)
Shop in Cork, Ireland. Made flintlock
duelling pistols and 'screw-off' cannon
barrel flintlock pistols.

Length: 8 in.
Barrel length: 2¾ in.
Bore: 0.45 in.

The lock of this pocket pistol is of round section and is slightly banana shaped. There is no bridle to the frizzen, nor to the tumbler inside the lock. The stock itself is of darkly figured walnut. The barrel is in the form of a cannon barrel, especially attractive in view of its small dimensions, and is of the type known as 'turn off', or 'screw barrel'. The furniture, including the trigger-guard, serpentine sideplate and rounded butt-cap, are all of brass.

Engraving consists of 'Whitney', on the lockplate, with 'Cork' on the breech in Roman lettering. Proof marks are of early London type.

A special feature of this pistol is that the barrel tang is secured by a screw passing through the stock from below, the screw head being concealed beneath the trigger-guard. This is found on early pistols.

There are no replacement parts on this weapon, which has an overall brown patina, due to the effects of polishing on light rust over a period of years.

The lack of a bridle to the frizzen, and also to the tumbler, dates this weapon to around 1740, or even earlier.

Early flintlock pocket pistol by Whitney, with pincer type bullet mould incorporating sprue cutter

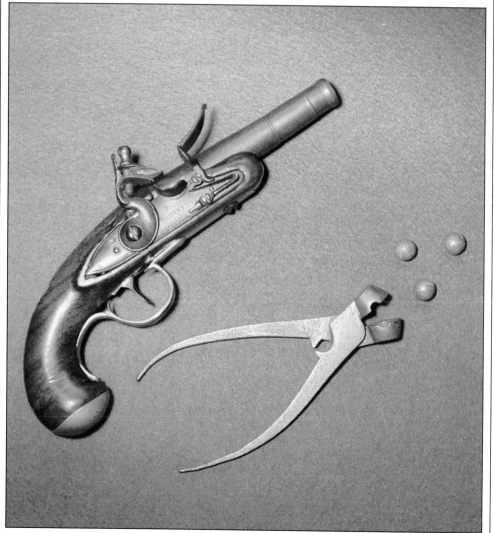

Pair of Percussion Belt Pistols by Smith

SMITH (1830–1850)
Shop at Braintree. Made double-barrelled percussion pistols. Also cased percussion belt pistols with accessories.

Some time ago I acquired this pair of percussion pistols in their original red-velvet-lined and fitted case.

The case itself was the finest I have ever seen, being of highly polished and unblemished mahogany, with brassbound corners and a beautifully shaped escutcheon in the lid.

The guns themselves were percussion boxlock pistols with dolphin-shaped sidehammers. Most of the original browning was present on the octagonal twist barrels. The nipple bolsters contained a screw which could be removed for easy cleaning. The ramrods were of swivel type and were of blued steel. Belt hooks were fitted to the left side of each weapon.

Stocks were of walnut, with flared and finely chequered butts, containing traps to hold spare percussion caps. The maker's name and address was engraved on the upper barrel flat, and all the steel furniture retained the original charcoal blueing. The case compartments contained the usual accessories for loading and cleaning the weapons, and, like the guns themselves, were in near-new condition.

The entire outfit represented the very best in gunsmithing and casing techniques.

Pair of Queen Anne Flintlock Pistols by Delany

DELANY, H. (1690–1750)
Shop in London. Made officers' flintlock holster pistols and flintlock blunderbusses. Also made Queen Anne-type flintlock cannon-barrelled pistols.

Length: 8¾ in.
Barrel length: 3½ in.
Bore: 0.45 in.

This is a magnificent example of a pair of Queen Anne cannon-barrelled flintlock pistols of intermediate form. The mechanism is boxlock, with centre-swung hammers, the cocks of swan-neck shape. The stocks are of dark, figured walnut, and are inlaid with silver wiring in scroll pattern. The ball butt terminates in a silver grotesque mask butt-cap. 'Delany' is engraved on the left side of the frame, in Roman lettering, with 'London' on the other. The barrels are engraved on the upper surfaces with consecutive Police registration marks. Proof marks are of the early Birmingham private variety.

The weapons themselves have a dark overall patination, while the barrels are of the 'turn off' variety, being unscrewed for loading.

This type of pistol was a development of the 'true' Queen Anne pistol, with its sidehammer boxlock construction, before it adopted its final form, with a slabsided butt and centre-swung hammer.

These pistols are of the highest quality, and date from about 1750.

Pair of Queen Anne style flintlock pistols with cannon barrels, by Charles Delany

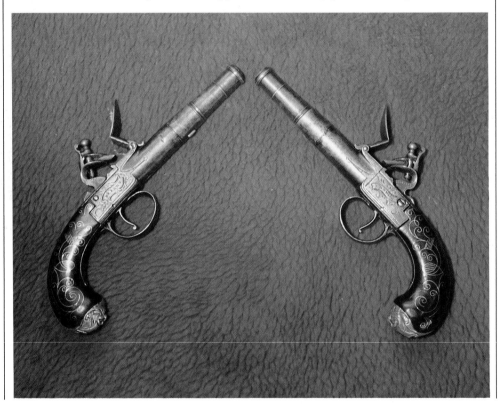

Flintlock Pocket Pistol by Perry

> **PERRY, William** (*c.* 1780)
> Shop in Birmingham. Made flintlock
> brass-barrelled pocket pistols and
> flintlock cannon-barrelled pistols. Also
> made brass-barrelled flintlock
> blunderbusses.

Length: 6 in.
Barrel length: 1¼ in.
Bore: 0.38 in.

This cannon-barrelled pistol of small dimensions is the finest example of its type I have ever seen.

The boxlock mechanism is of the centre-swung hammer variety. The slabsided walnut butt is entirely inlaid with silver wiring in scrolling form. The walnut butt is light in colour, and bears the initials, presumably of its former owner, 'E.D.' These initials are impressed on the stock below the backstrap. The tiny cannon barrel is of exquisite form. Surprisingly, it is not a 'turn off' barrel, but is loaded at the muzzle in the normal way. Engraving comprises trophies of arms on either side of the frame, while a cartouche on the left side bears the name 'Perry', in Roman lettering. Proof marks are probably early Birmingham private type, and consist of crossed sceptres crowned, although these marks could represent Tower proof marks for private weapons. The overall finish is of dull steel, which presents a very attractive appearance. A special feature of the weapon is the safety catch, which is operated by sliding forward the trigger-guard with the pistol at half cock, effectively locking the mainspring.

Although by a little-known provincial gunsmith, this pocket cannon-barrelled pistol is of top quality, indicating that high standards of craftsmanship were not the sole prerogative of the London makers.

Notes on the Duel

'It has a strange quick jar upon the ear,
That cocking of a pistol, when you know
A moment more will bring its sight to
  bear
Upon your person, twelve yards off or
  so.'

                                    BYRON

The conduct of the duel followed well-established guidelines, which were set out in a pamphlet entitled *The British Code of Duel*.

The equivalent work in Ireland was entitled *The Clonmel Regulations*, while on the Continent it was the *Code Duello*.

When a challenge was issued and accepted, it was customary to appoint one or two seconds, who were empowered to act on one's behalf. It was their duty to meet in order to try to effect a reconciliation but, if this could not be achieved, an arrangement would be made to meet at dawn on the following day.

The parties would arrive separately and a further attempt to resolve the matter peacefully would be made by the seconds. If this could not be concluded satisfactorily, a case of duelling pistols would be produced, and loaded carefully under the watchful eyes of the seconds.

The distance at which the duel was to be fought would be decided upon. This was usually ten to fifteen paces. The signal would then be agreed upon – usually a shouted command or clap of the hands.

The order of firing was also important, whether it be firing simultaneously, at will, or, as sometimes happened, with the injured party firing first.

Sometimes honour was satisfied by the mere discharge of the pistols, but on other occasions honour required that blood be drawn, or even that one man lie dead on the field. In the latter case, the weapons would be reloaded as often as necessary to achieve this dreadful outcome.

Gentlemen were encouraged to practise their shooting skills at their clubs, whilst helpful manuals were produced as guides to prospective combatants.

One was instructed to aim at the fleshy part of the upper thigh, as such a wound would rupture the femoral artery with probably fatal consequences. On the other hand, a high shot would enter the abdominal or chest cavities, with equally poor prospects for the recipient, whereas even a low shot would fracture the femur and bring down one's opponent.

The style of shooting was rather different from the two-handed method now favoured by police marksmen.

The right elbow was bent, the arm protecting the chest and the hand held well up over the face. The duellist turned his side towards his adversary, with the stomach drawn well in, in order to present the smallest possible target.

Fortunately, public opinion turned against this once honourable activity, and the whole question of duelling fell into public ridicule and disrepute.

Pair of duelling pistols by Durs Egg

Flintlock Duelling Pistol by Ross

ROSS (*c.* 1810)
Shop at Edinburgh, Scotland. Made
double-barrel flintlock fowling pieces.
Also flintlock duelling pistols and
percussion target pistols of fine
workmanship.

Length: 15½ in.
Barrel length: 9½ in.
Bore: 0.56 in.

This weapon is undoubtedly the finest example of a duelling pistol I have ever come across. I missed the opportunity of acquiring it when it first appeared in circulation, being on holiday. However, I knew that it had gone to a dealer of my acquaintance, who was not really interested in the weapon as such and, after some years, being on friendly terms with this man, I gave him a handsome profit and added it to my collection.

The lock and cock were of flat section. The pan was of the 'rainproof' variety, and a roller bearing was fitted to the toe of the frizzen spring. The lock, cock and frizzen retaining their original case hardening. The weapon had no 'set' trigger; this device was a feature of many high-quality duelling pistols and allowed the weapon to be fired by the merest touch of the trigger. It was 'set' either by pushing the trigger forwards or by adjustment of a small capstan screw in front of the trigger. The device is sometimes referred to as a 'hair' trigger.

The pistol was half stocked, the beautiful walnut stock having a finely chequered butt and a horn fore-end. The octagonal 9½-inch barrel retained its entire original browning intact. The vent was lined with platinum and one gold line was inlaid at the breech. The barrel had, as in all duelling pistols, a silver foresight and a V-shaped rear-sight. The trigger-guard and ramrod pipes were of blued steel. The maker's name, 'Ross', was engraved on the lockplate. Proof marks were of the post-1813 Birmingham variety.

I tried for many years to find its companion pistol, since undoubtedly it was one of a pair, and in the course of time met a former owner, who had had the pistol since childhood. He, too, had sought the other pistol, but was convinced that it had been lost for ever, and eventually I had to abandon the search. Sometimes, in the disposal of large estates, it used to be the practice to divide a case of duelling pistols between two sons, and I have come across several examples of this. Perhaps this was the fate of the missing pistol.

Flintlock duelling pistol by Ross of Edinburgh in magnificent condition

Cased Flintlock Duelling Pistols by Egg

EGG, Durs (1770–1834)
Shop at 1 Pall Mall, London. Celebrated
London gunsmith. Had the Royal
Warrant. Made Ferguson breech-loading
rifles. Also made over-and-under
flintlock double-barrelled pistols and
fine-quality cased flintlock duelling
pistols.

It is, I believe, the ambition of every collector of antique firearms to own a cased pair of flintlock duelling pistols.

I wanted to obtain an outfit which was original in every respect, and in the best condition possible, but to do this meant trading in several pistols in exchange.

As by this time I had virtually completed my military collection, and was moving on, as it were, to civilian weapons, I chose to part with almost all of my military flintlocks, and was well satisfied with my end of the bargain, as, in all fairness, was the dealer with his.

After all, I was pleased to make a new and prestigious acquisition, while no doubt he would make a handsome profit from the exchange, and, of course, this is what any deal is all about, each party to a deal having something to gain from the transaction.

The duellers are cased in a large mahogany case, with a brass drop handle inserted in the lid. There are two locking catches at the front.

The case itself is now highly polished, but shows evidence of a considerable amount of wear from having lain around, neglected, perhaps in a workshop or storeroom where other objects would be thrown on top. It is lined with faded red velvet. Both guns are in magnificent condition, having 9½-inch octagonal barrels which retain all their original browning, revealing the beautiful twist pattern created by their method of construction. The locks and cocks are of flat section. There is an ingenious safety device, formed by the rear of the lockplate, which is a separate piece, and slides forward to operate on half cock. The pan is semi-rainproof in type. There is no set trigger. The locks, cocks, frizzens, top-jaws and screws all retain their original case hardening. A roller is attached to the toe of the frizzen to speed the pan opening. The weapons are half stocked, with horn fore-ends. The stocks are of walnut, and highly polished. They have hockey stick-shaped butts, with crisp chequering, and teardrop finials at the rear of the lock and the corresponding part on the opposite side, behind the sidenail. Both ramrods are brass tipped, one plain, the other fitted with a worm and cap. The barrels have a silver foresight and V-shaped rear sight. The blued barrel wedges have rectangular silver escutcheons, and another silver escutcheon, behind the barrel tang, is engraved 'A.H.'. The exquisitely engraved trigger-guards have pineapple finials, and are concave at the rear to accommodate the third finger more easily. The engraving is so sharp, that running one's finger over it almost scratches the skin. The lockplate is engraved 'D.Egg', in script, and the barrel 'London', in Roman lettering. There is restrained engraving of the lockplates and cocks. The weapons bear consecutively numbered Dublin Castle registration marks. London proof marks are stamped under the barrels. Both pistols are of the finest quality.

Enclosed within the case are a number of accessories, all in mint condition, some of steel and others of brass. There is a two-piece duelling pistol cleaning rod, made of rosewood, with several cleaning jags. One tool is of a pattern I have never seen before, and is obviously designed to remove powder fouling from the bore. There is a three-armed turnscrew and also a vent pricker. An interesting accessory is the black leather flint wallet, which Egg liked to use in casing his duelling pistols. It contains its six original sharpened flints.

I have studied many cases by Durs Egg and have found that he often used fluted three-way powder flasks. The one in this set is of this type and is in mint condition, with an undamaged case and original blued cut-off spring. It still contains black powder. There are also, of course, compartments to hold balls and spare flints. A number of balls are present in another compartment, showing considerable and genuine ageing, together with a small amount of wadding, another spare flint and several waxed patches to aid in loading. Yet another compartment contains the ball mould and a rare and original pan cleaning brush. Finally there are the case key and an original mainspring clamp.

Whilst there is no trade label in the lid this is of the padded variety, and one would not expect to find a label in this type of lid.

It is of some importance, however, for the collector to determine whether or not case and guns belong together.

Thus, one must examine case and guns very closely, lifting the weapons to see if there are pressure marks and, if so, that these are in the correct places. Does the wear seem excessive, or not enough? One must lift the flask and look below, and again determine if pressure marks of

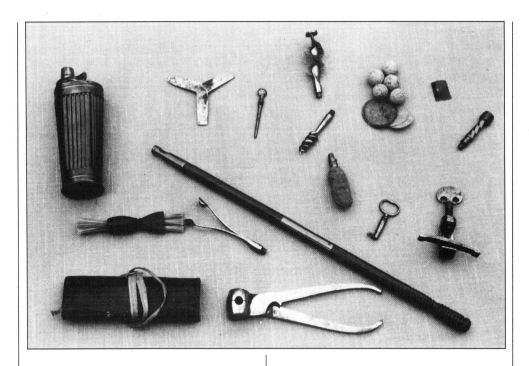

Top left: *Cased pair of flintlock duelling pistols by Durs Egg*

Bottom left: *Close-up of lock*

Above: *Accessories cased with Durs Egg pistols*

appropriate depth and situation are present. The lid lining must be inspected – are there markings due to the impingeing of the pistols and the ivory lid buttons on the cloth, and are these in the correct positions? Are there other markings on the linings which cannot be explained? Are the accessories correct? Were these the type used by the particular maker?

I believe that, provided contemporary accessories are used, that is to say, accessories of the period, then it is of no real moment if they were not originally in the case.

However, I am 100 per cent satisfied that my guns and accessories are authentic in every respect. I have, nevertheless, set out how the inexperienced collector should go about things if he wishes to acquire a cased set.

I always remember that, not long after I started collecting, I wanted to buy a cased set. I examined several, but really I was at a total loss, because I just didn't know how to go about it.

In fact, I almost purchased a pair of officer's percussion presentation pistols in a case with several accessories, but I am very glad I didn't make the purchase, because I am quite certain now that these had been 'cased up', as it is called, and were not the sort of guns that the discerning collector would wish to have.

The answer for the novice collector of antique guns is, of course, to take a more experienced collector with him, because, as I have indicated, only an expert can tell, and even he is fallible.

Percussion Belt Pistol by Henneker

HENNEKER, E. E. (1832–1850)
Shop at Chatham, Kent. Made cased
percussion pistols with belt hooks. Also
percussion holster pistols with swivel
ramrods.

Length: 9½ in.
Barrel length: 5 in.
Bore: 0.65 in.

The lock of this pistol is known as 'back action', which signifies that the mainspring is behind the tumbler and pulls up on it by means of a short stirrup. A sliding safety engages the hammer at half cock. The weapon is full stocked to the muzzle, the walnut stock being highly polished and its butt finely chequered. There is a swivel ramrod. The twist barrel is octagonal in section, and incorporates a silver foresight and V-shaped rear sight. The maker's name is engraved in Roman lettering on the lockplate, and both the hammer and lockplate are scroll engraved. Proof marks are of late London type. A special feature of this weapon is the belt hook, which is fitted to the opposite side from the lock. There are no stock repairs or replacement parts whatsoever on this gun, although the barrel has been rebrowned and the nipple replaced.

Inside the lock the working parts are as bright and highly polished as the day they were first made – a really precision piece of workmanship. This large-bore weapon, known as a 'manstopper', was the first in my collection, and can truly be said to have started my search for antique firearms. This weapon was almost certainly purchased originally by a naval officer.

114

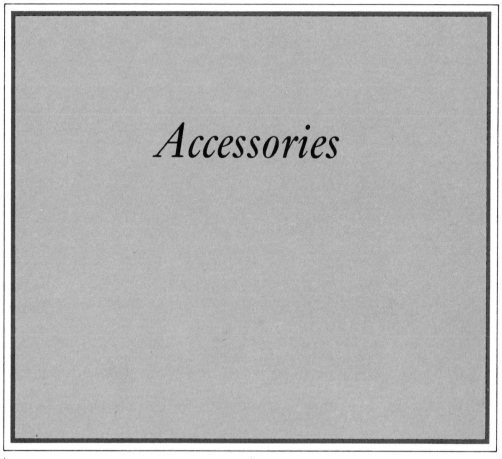

Accessories

Accessories of antique weapons constitute all the various accoutrements necessary to service them, and include powder flasks, be they gun or pistol flasks, powder measures, cappers, tins of percussion caps, nipple keys, turnscrews and a host of gun tools of every description.

They are fast disappearing, as more and more collectors look around them, and pick up an item here and another there, to place in a cased set, and so lose it forever.

The time is approaching when such accessories will be totally unobtainable and, in order to find any accessories, reproductions will have to be purchased.

This has already happened, to some extent, with the powder flask. Not so many years ago, almost every antique shop one visited had two or three gunflasks, albeit a bit dented, or perhaps with the spring missing, or a split seam. Arms fairs had half a dozen good flasks on nearly every stall. Today, however, a very different picture emerges, and at a recent fair, of perhaps forty or fifty flasks

90 per cent were reproductions, some very cleverly distressed to appear to be original.

I have always been fascinated by accessories, which I have acquired in all sorts of places, many being unrecognized for what they really were.

Only recently I found an original and rare two-piece duelling pistol cleaning rod, and purchased it, unrecognized, for £3, when, just a few stalls away, reproductions of the same item were selling for many times that figure. And this is true of many accessories.

One can still come across some excellent items, but it is rare to find a gun or pistol flask nowadays in original condition. Mostly, such flasks have gone into collections, or have been cased up with sets of pistols.

With accessories, one does not have to spend a great deal of money to build up a collection. For example, a tin of percussion caps can be bought from £4 upwards, and even such a collection alone can become quite varied and interesting after a few years.

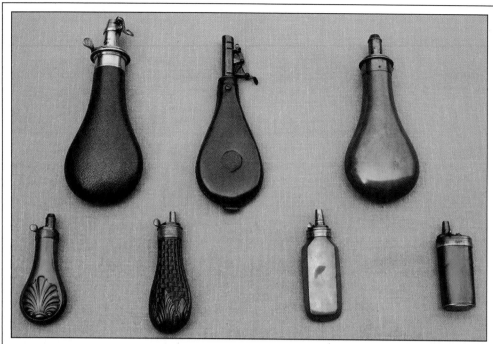

Powder flasks. In the upper row, the first is leather covered, and the middle one is a shot bag, whilst in the bottom row, the flasks are designed for pistols or revolvers. That on the right is a three-way flask, with compartments for ball, powder and, in this case, percussion caps, although the latter compartment could be used for flints

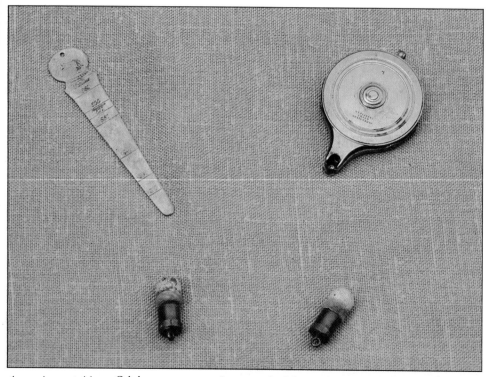

Accessories comprising a Colt bore gauge, percussion capper by Sykes, and two rare dustbin cartridges

116

Various examples of percussion cap tins. The oval variety is somewhat rare, and is made of pewter

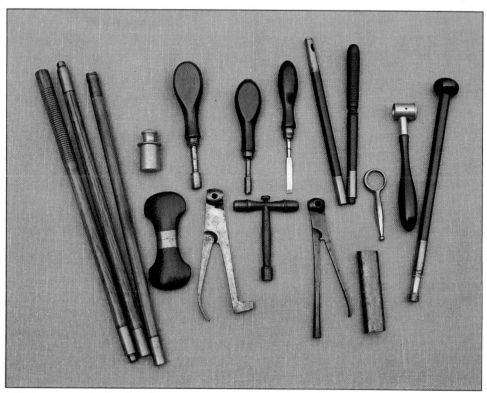

Various accessories of antique firearms

Conversions

Nipple keys and turnscrews are also becoming very difficult to find, and it is the fortunate collector who stumbles across these.

Leather shot bags are also interesting items, but these too, are being reproduced in large numbers, and after appropriate distressing would be very hard to recognize.

Powder measures, which were produced in large quantities, are, however, still in abundance, while pincer-type bullet moulds are also readily obtainable. One of the rarest items of all is the gun or pistol case, now practically extinct, and should a happy collector come across any, the asking price is liable to provoke a cardiac arrest.

With the advent of the percussion system there was an immediate demand for the new weapons, which were very much superior to the flintlocks, which they replaced.

Many people, however, preferred to retain their flintlock weapons, but had them converted to the new system.

This conversion is carried out in various ways. In a sidelock flintlock, the method consisted of removing the frizzen and spring, filling the three holes created by means of a peg or screw filed flat with the surface of the lockplate and cutting away the pan. The cock was then replaced by a hammer, and the vent tapped to receive a steel drum into which a nipple could be screwed. This is the so-called drum and nipple conversion.

This type of conversion is often fairly crude, since the drum is never in close apposition to the new contour of the upper part of the lock.

The job was frequently carried out by a gunsmith of lesser quality than the original maker, and this can be detected by comparison of the engraving with that on the rest of the weapon. Occasionally, however, these conversions are of excellent quality, and the drum and hammer are engraved in perfect harmony with the other engraving.

The best way of converting a sidelock flintlock to percussion is undoubtedly the insertion of new breeching, and such conversions do not offend the critical eye. The tell-tale filled holes and the style of the lockplate both give the game away, however.

With boxlock flintlocks, the frizzen and boss are removed, the frizzen spring recess filled and the vent tapped to receive a nipple. The cock is then replaced by a hammer.

Sometimes, in later pistols, this conversion can be difficult to detect, but careful examination will always reveal the true state of affairs.

It was not uncommon, with a pair of pocket pistols, to convert only one in the above manner; with the second pistol, instead of removing the cock, an abbreviated hammer was fitted between the jaws, and I have even encountered examples in which the frizzen has not been removed but, after slight alteration, serves as a convenient nipple protector.

The great difficulty, for the collector, is not so much in spotting conversions but in detecting when they have been 'put back', that is, reconverted into flintlocks in order to increase their value.

Thus it is necessary, when purchasing any flintlock, to examine the lock area very carefully. Look at the frizzen to see whether it has been marked by the flint over the years, and try to decide if these marks are genuine. Now examine the pan to see if it appears new. In genuine flintlocks this area often shows evidence of corrosion. Sometimes the inside of the lock reveals evidence of welding. Frequently, with a reconversion, the cock may not be of quite the correct pattern, the frizzen just a shade less elegant than it might be. Check that the engraving is of the same style and depth as that on the rest of the weapon. The number of reconversions is not, of course, very high, but nevertheless one should tread very carefully.

I believe that conversions are an important stage in the development of antique firearms, and should be accepted by the collector as such.

Caveat Emptor

I remember being in Scotland on a foraging trip, and stumbling across a very rare powder flask in an antique shop. It was an Ames 'Peace flask', and I knew it was very valuable. I purchased it for £18.

In those days, although I no longer subscribe to that view, I used to clean every powder flask that came into my possession, and then allow it to tarnish naturally.

This, I felt, gave it a uniformity of finish which would mellow over the following months.

I therefore started to clean this flask, which was tarnished and had deeply ingrained dirt in its contours, but was a trifle surprised at the ease with which the accumulated dirt of years was removed.

When I returned to England, I passed through a small town where I knew there was an antique shop, and going over to look in the window I was horrified to see another Ames Peace flask, this one, however, being bright and clean. Now, discovering one such rare flask would be the find of a lifetime, but two would be nothing short of miraculous.

I entered the shop and asked the proprietor, 'Is that flask a reproduction?' She was indignant. 'Most certainly not,' she said, 'when I got the flask it was filthy, and I've treated it with acid to clean it up like that.'

The penny dropped, and I beat a hasty retreat. Later, I found that these flasks were being reproduced in large numbers, and sold off, one here and one there, around the country.

I sent the flask back to the antique shop where I'd found it and, being very genuine dealers, they refunded my money, saying that they had believed the flask to be completely genuine, and I have no reason to doubt this.

On another occasion I purchased a Tower Sea-service pistol. The story was that, somewhere in England, a couple of barrels had been discovered. When the seals were broken, inside were dozens of Tower Sea-service pistols, all covered in their original grease preservative, and in completely original and unfired condition. It was said, however, that the guns were not of first quality. The stocks were liberally stamped with the proof marks beloved of collectors of antique military weapons.

When I was offered one, it seemed to me to be genuine in all respects, after all, the proof marks were obviously Tower ones, and were clearly stamped on the breech as well as the stock. I could see, however, that the gun was not, as stated, of first quality. I therefore showed the weapon to my old mentor, Fred Tomlinson. As usual, he turned it over and over, and as usual my face fell. 'This gun is this year's model,' he said at last. I was incredulous. How could this possibly be?

He pulled out a screwdriver and removed the huge screw attaching the butt-cap to the stock.

'This is the only way you can tell,' he said, indicating the tell-tale electric weld across the shank of the screw where the large screwhead had been attached for ease of construction.

Of course, electric arc welding could not be contemporary with a weapon purporting to be early 19th century.

I returned this pistol to the seller. After that, I removed the butt-cap screws of every Tower pistol in my possession!

The collector is fortunate indeed who has not been caught out by cleverly aged reproductions. This applies to accessories as well as to antique guns.

One always feels cheated on such occasions, perhaps made worse by the fact that one has failed to recognize these fakes for what they are – that we have been tested and found wanting. It is essential to shrug off such incidents as inevitable, and to try not to be too depressed by such setbacks to our collecting.

We should certainly not yield to the temptation of abandoning our chosen hobby.

One only learns through experience, and such episodes broaden our knowledge and, although dispiriting and costly, remind us to be more wary in the future.

Once, at an arms fair in Leeds, I purchased a bronze-framed percussion pistol with a fluted barrel. The light at the fair had been very dim, and when I arrived home, I took the pistol into the garden to show it off to my wife.

When I saw the pistol in the bright sunlight, however, I nearly died. The stock barely fitted around the barrel tang, and there was stain and plastic wood everywhere.

I felt like throwing the gun into the dustbin, and it had cost a good deal of money.

When I had calmed down, I worked out a plan to restore the stock of the weapon. It was a laborious job, necessitating the removal of all traces of the previous repairwork and doing the job again, but properly. When I had finished the work it was undetectable, even in the brightest sunlight.

Such a restoration is, and must be, totally acceptable. It does not, in my opinion, represent faking in any way, and consists merely in bringing the gun back to its original status.

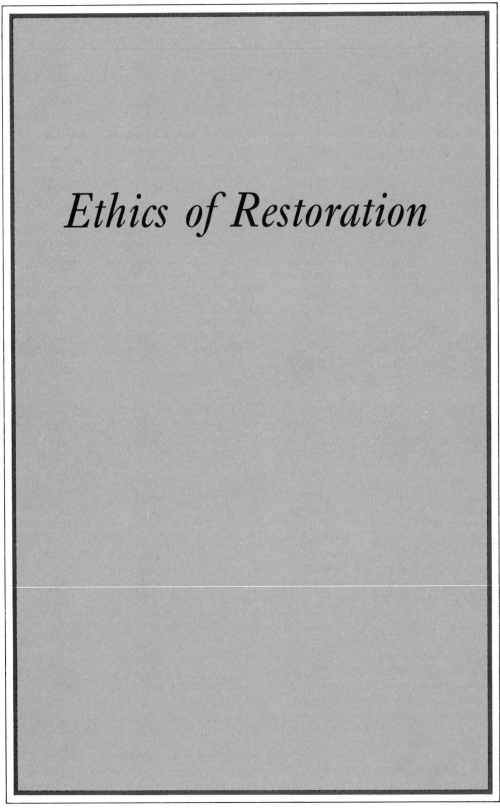

Ethics of Restoration

Throughout this book the reader will have noticed that I have made a great deal of reference to the restoration of antique firearms.

Opinions are divided among collectors as to what constitutes restoration. Some purists feel that no parts should be replaced, and that even gunstocks should be left shattered, or with cracks, or pieces missing. Such individuals feel that replacement parts when fitted should not be aged, so that it is obvious to all that the part is a replacement.

To my mind, this is arrant nonsense. Guns, say the purists, may be collected, but only rare and valuable undamaged pieces, which the average collector cannot afford.

Those who subscribe to these views must be either very wealthy or have started collecting guns many years ago. What they cannot understand is that the ordinary collector cannot, in the main, afford to collect such valuable pieces. He is forced to deal at the lower end of the market.

Is he, then, to hang up pieces on his walls with broken stocks and missing hammers?

The answer is shatteringly obvious. The average collector wants his pieces to look as attractive as those he sees in museums, and, to this end, his weapons must be restored. But they must be restored properly, with parts as near to the original as can possibly be found. And, once replaced, these parts must be blended to match the rest of the gun.

This is in no sense faking, but constitutes proper and methodical restoration.

I have restored many, many items in this way, and each time I feel a tremendous sense of achievement.

A very good friend of mine, and a collector of antique firearms, used to work very painstakingly on his weapons. The metal parts would be filed and sanded smooth to remove the slightest trace of pitting. They would then be polished bright. Stocks would be repaired, dents removed, splits and holes filled, then sanded smooth as satin; the end result was an antique gun which looked as though it had just come off the production line.

This is the direct antithesis of what I have tried to achieve in my endeavours to restore antique guns. His work is meticulous, but in my opinion falls short of complete restoration.

When replacing missing accessories in cased sets, so long as these are the sorts of items normally found with the particular weapons, I think that such replacements are infinitely preferable to having empty compartments, and I would even go so far as to say that casing a gun or guns, provided that this is not done to deceive but merely to re-create the conditions obtaining when the weapons were originally sold, is perfectly legitimate; the better the casing, the more authentic the result.

Restoring antique weapons gives a wonderful sense of achievement and satisfaction. What a pity that the number of unrestored weapons is now diminishing rapidly and that the talents accumulated by many older collectors are now lying largely neglected.

History

The history of antique firearms begins in the 11th century with the discovery of gunpowder. It is not known with certainty where this discovery was made, although my own preference is for China, as the Chinese were very skilled in the production of fireworks, and it seems likely that the explosive qualities of gunpowder were discovered in that country.

The earliest reference to gunpowder occurs in a treatise of the mid-13th century, when a Franciscan monk named Roger Bacon wrote down the formula for gunpowder.

Interestingly, this formula, containing the essential ingredients of charcoal, sulphur and saltpetre, was written in code, which survived unbroken until successfully deciphered by Partington in the early years of this century.

How the propulsive properties of gunpowder were discovered is uncertain, but it is likely that the Arabs, who traded extensively with China, brought back the new gunpowder with them, and began to produce primitive weapons for the first time.

The earliest dated picture of a gun can be found in the manuscript of Walter de Milemete, who was the tutor of Edward III. This picture is dated 1326. The gun in question is a bronze, vase-shaped object, the projectile being an iron arrow.

Above: *Arquebusier from de Gheyn engraving of 1607.* Smithsonian Institution, Washington
Below: *de Milemete manuscript – 1326, the earliest dated picture of a gun.* Christ Church, Oxford

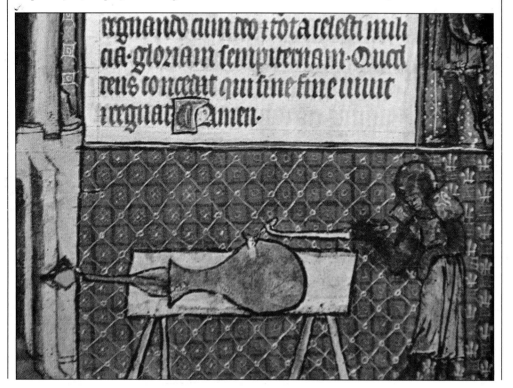

Gradually, shortened versions began to be constructed, and were attached to sticks or staves, to form the earliest handguns; a few of these early weapons have survived, and are to be found in some of the more important collections in the world, such as that in the Tower of London.

The earliest battle at which cannon were known to have been used was the battle of Crécy in 1346, and an eyewitness account has been written of that battle, describing the terrible destructive effect of cannon on that occasion.

The next stage in the development of firearms was the invention, in the 15th century, of the matchlock. This was a heavy weapon with a long iron barrel, which had to be fired supported on a rest. It was loaded by pouring a charge of powder and ball down the muzzle. At the breech end of the gun was a shallow recess called a pan. This communicated with the main charge in the breech by means of a vent or touchhole. The pan was primed with fine priming powder. Also at the breech end of the gun was an S-shaped piece of metal, called a serpentine. To this was attached a lighted match, or cord, soaked in a solution of saltpetre. The match was lit at both ends, in case one end should be extinguished in battle. The serpentine was brought forward, firstly manually and later by means of a trigger, thereby causing the powder in the pan to ignite, so setting off the main charge.

The matchlock was a very robust and depend-able weapon, and was to last, in certain remote parts of the world at least, for several hundred years.

In the 16th century, the wheel-lock was discovered. This came from two main centres in Germany, Augsburg and Nuremberg. It worked on the principle of the modern cigarette lighter. A piece of iron pyrites was held against a serrated iron wheel, which was made to rotate rapidly against it, producing a shower of sparks which could ignite the powder in the pan.

The wheel-lock was a superb weapon, and is known as the mechanic's delight. It was, however, somewhat delicate, and tended to be used to arm élite groups of men, such as bodyguards of princes and kings or private armies employed by noblemen.

Wheel-locks were also used extensively as hunting rifles. Surviving examples tend to be embellished with gold, silver, ivory or bone inlay, and are often museum pieces, rather than in the hands of the average collector.

In 1625, a Frenchman called Marin le Bourgeoys, who was gunmaker to Louis XIII, discovered the flintlock, sometimes known as the French lock.

The flintlock was a very reliable weapon, and was to last for 200 years.

A piece of flint, held in the jaws of the cock, was

Close-up of wheel-lock

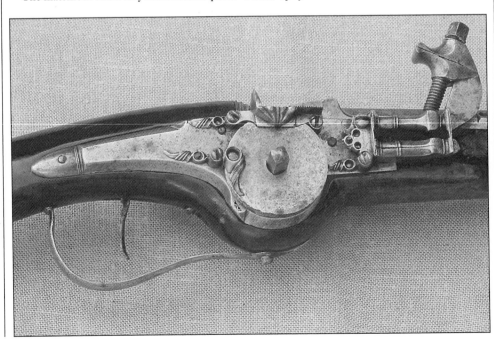

allowed to strike an L-shaped pan cover, called the frizzen, sending a shower of sparks into the pan at the touch of a trigger. Two minor variations were, firstly, the snaphaunce, in which the pan cover and striking mechanism were separate, and, secondly, the miquelet lock, which had an external mainspring and a ring-shaped top-jaw screw. Miquelet locks were a feature of Spanish weapons.

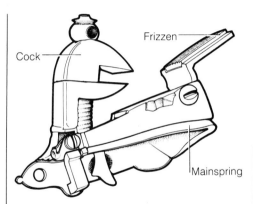

MIQUELET LOCK

Flintlock weapons had two principal drawbacks. One was a tendency to 'hang fire', this being the split second of delay after the powder in the pan ignites and before the ignition of the main charge. This was of some importance to shooters of duck and game, since the quarry was able to see

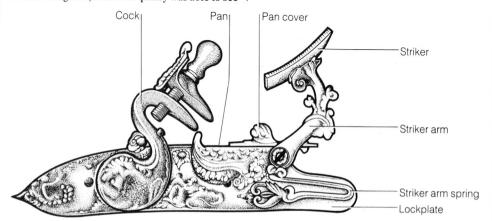

SNAPHAUNCE LOCK

this 'flash in the pan', and take evasive action.

The other drawback of the flintlock was, of course, the constant danger of the priming powder in the pan becoming damp, thus rendering the gun useless.

It had been known for more than a century that fulminates, that is to say, salts of certain elements, notably antimony and mercury, when struck sharply, produced an explosion but, for some unaccountable reason, no one had thought of applying this to the firearms industry.

A Scottish minister, Alexander John Forsyth, of the parish of Belhelvie, near Aberdeen, experimented with fulminates and, with the co-operation of Lord Moira, who was Master of the Ordnance, worked for two years in the Tower of London. With the replacement of Lord Moira at the Tower, Forsyth was told to leave, but formed an association with a well-known London gunsmith, Purdey, and in 1807, took out a patent for a lock which utilized fulminate of mercury as a detonator.

Forsyth finally returned to the ministry at

Alexander John Forsyth, inventor of the percussion system. HM Tower of London

Belhelvie, but will be recognized forever as the father of the percussion system. It was left, however, to an English emigrant artist called Joshua Shaw to perfect the invention, with the discovery of the percussion cap, patented in Philadelphia in 1822. It consisted of a small copper cap, in the base of which was a small amount of fulminate of mercury covered over with tinfoil and shellac. When the cap was placed on a nipple and was struck by the hammer of a gun, an explosion resulted which could set off the main charge.

The percussion system was thought to be more dependable, faster firing and harder hitting than flintlock weapons, and soon people began to convert their weapons to the new system.

It was not long before attempts began to be made to produce a revolver, which really became practical for the first time with the discovery of the percussion cap.

It was an American called Samuel Colt who made the breakthrough in 1836, with the invention of a revolver which, although not entirely satisfactory, was nevertheless a big improvement on previous attempts.

After the redesigning of the weapon during the Mexican War of 1846, Colt opened a factory in Hartford, Connecticut, and began to produce percussion revolvers in large numbers.

His weapons were robust, having few working parts, and revolutionized the firearms industry.

Many attempts were made to evade Colt's patent, but none could match the Colt for accuracy or dependability.

Colt's main rival was an Englishman called Robert Adams, who had invented a revolver considered by many to be superior to the Colt. It is true that the Adams, after modification in 1854 which allowed it to be fired either single or double action, was more suited to the British Army in the wars of that time, being of larger calibre than the Colt and faster firing.

In 1855, a man called Rollin White patented the first metallic cartridge.

This was simply a charge of powder, ball and percussion cap, all in one self-contained unit, but it was a tremendous advance, since it made loading very much easier. No longer would one

Samuel Colt, inventor of the first practical revolver.
Bettman Archive/BBC Hulton Picture Library

have to fumble with percussion caps in the frenzied heat of battle, or when one's fingers were numb with cold, but could merely load the cartridge into the revolver through a gate in the rear of the cylinder.

The first cartridges were rim-fire, but this was soon altered to centre-fire, and it is interesting to speculate that today, 130 years later, centre-fire cartridges are still in use in the modern revolver.

With the advent of the metallic cartridge, the percussion era came to an end, and so, too, does the history of antique firearms, cartridge weapons being beyond the scope of this work.

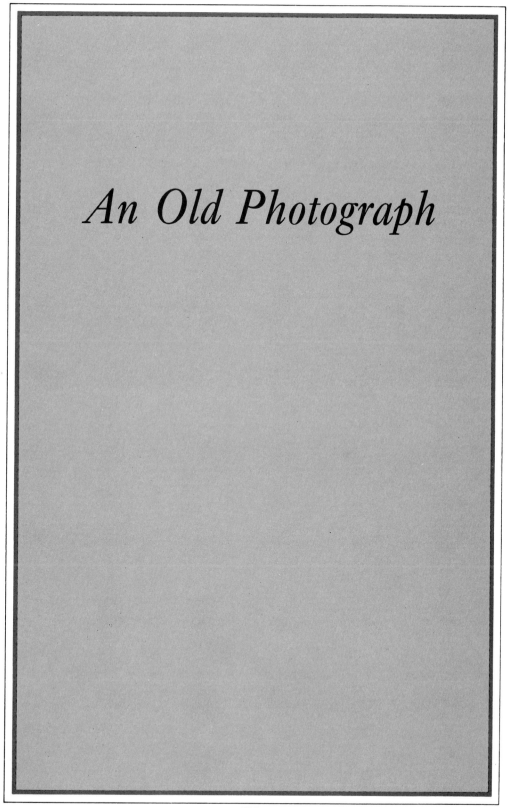

An Old Photograph

The photograph reproduced below was taken many years ago, by a proud collector of antique weapons.

It is easy to see that the collector's home was a very modest one. The old-fashioned radio and the style of decoration suggest a date in the 1930s. The electrical wiring seems to be quite primitive, and the washing can be seen hanging on a clothes pulley.

The collection of weapons hanging on the wall, however, is quite staggering, and in sharp contrast to the poor surroundings.

It comprises three wheel-lock rifles, one a Tschinke, an early flintlock fowling piece with skeleton stock, a blunderbuss, a rare and high-quality Turkish miquelet lock rifle, a sword pistol, two cannon igniters, four Queen Anne flintlock pistols, two wheel-lock pistols, one with a ball butt, the other flared, and the rest an assortment of early flintlock pistols of various types and sizes.

Not one of the weapons had required the slightest degree of restoration. Each was in pristine condition, and in those far-off days had probably been acquired for a few shillings an item. What this must have entailed in terms of sacrifice at that time is hard to imagine; indeed, one wonders how such a fabulous collection could have been put together in such a household in that difficult period between the two world wars. I would estimate that the collection would be worth, in today's terms, in the region of £45,000.

An enviable collection

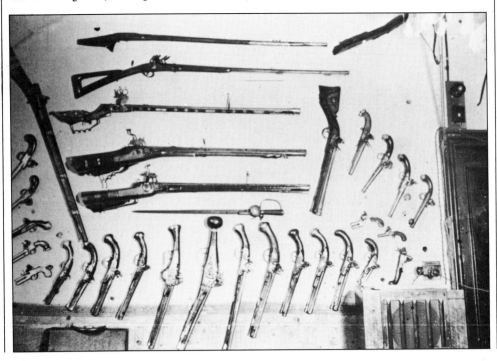

Proof Marks

Prior to 1638, the proving of weapons was carried out by two Honourable Companies, the Blacksmith's and the Armourer's. Their proof marks consisted, in the first instance, of a four-looped crown above an anvil, and in the second, of an 'A' surmounted by a similar crown.

With the establishment of the Gunmaker's Company in 1638, and the granting of a Royal Charter, the proving of weapons was carried out exclusively by that company, their proof marks consisting of an anagrammed 'G.P.', denoting Gunmaker's Proof, surmounted by a four-looped crown, and their view mark, a 'V' surmounted by a similar crown.

The method of proving barrels has already been discussed.

By 1702, the proof marks had been modified to consist of the letters 'G.P.', surmounted by a two-looped crown, while the view mark consisted of a crowned 'V', both marks being in oval recesses.

Another mark that sometimes appears on weapons is a crowned 'F', appearing between the view and proof marks. This denotes that the barrel-maker was a 'foreigner', that is to say, was not a member of the Gunmaker's Company, and indicates that the barrel was constructed after 1741. In addition, some gunsmiths preferred to use their own mark, normally their initials, as well as the standard London proof marks.

Post-1813 Birmingham Proof marks

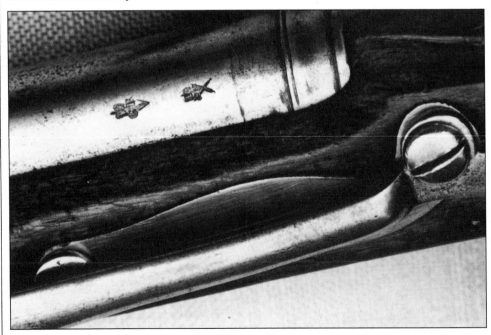

Tower Proof marks

132

The Birmingham Proof House was established in 1813. Prior to this date, individual makers had their own proof houses and proof marks. One such mark consisted of a crowned 'P' as the proof mark and a crowned 'V' as the view mark, usually in oval recesses.

Another such mark was a 'P' surmounting crossed sceptres, representing the proof mark, whilst the view mark was a 'V' surmounting crossed sceptres, both in oval recesses.

The Birmingham proof mark consisted of crossed sceptres surmounted by a crown, and the letters 'B.P.C.', the view mark being a crown surmounting crossed sceptres, and the letter 'V'.

Tower proof marks consisted of a crown surmounting crossed sceptres, view marks being a crowned Royal Cypher above a broad arrow.

Enfield markings consisted of crossed sceptres crowned, representing the proof mark, while the view mark was a crowned 'T.P.' above a broad arrow.

Occasionally, the collector will encounter arms which possess the same proof and view marks, consisting of crossed sceptres crowned. These marks represent the Tower proof and view marks for private arms, but may also represent the private marks of certain Birmingham makers prior to 1813.

Tower Proof marks for private arms

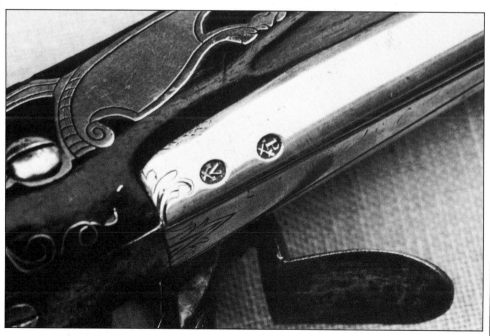

Early Birmingham Proof marks

133

The Complete Collection

It is virtually inevitable that the stage will eventually be reached when the collector of antique firearms will ask himself, 'Is my collection now complete? Have I bought my very last gun?'

I personally do not believe that the true collector ever achieves this ethereal goal, since the direction of his collecting urges is constantly changing. For example, my own collection has undergone many such alterations. Like most collectors, in the first flush of enthusiasm for my new hobby, I used to purchase almost anything and everything I could lay my eager hands on, but gradually I became more interested in acquiring weapons that had a military background. After a little while, the direction altered once more, as I began to dispose of my longarms and to concentrate exclusively on pistols made for civilian use.

Most collectors experience similar alterations in the direction and emphasis of their collections, some specializing in flintlock weapons, others in percussion guns; some will buy only brass-barrelled pistols, or weapons with silver mounts, others only long guns, pocket pistols or even duelling pistols. There is practically no end to the variations possible in the creation of a collection.

It will thus be apparent to the collector of antique firearms that, of necessity, not every type of gun is represented in my own collection as it exists today, or even in all the weapons that have at one time been part of it.

I would like, therefore, in order to correct this deficiency, to give some account of other common types of antique firearm that the reader is likely to come across, and which, for reasons of economy, space or inclination, do not form part of my own collection

Blunderbuss Pistols

These pistols are so named because of the flaring of the muzzle, sometimes referred to as 'swamping', or 'belling'. They are of two principal types, the first being smoothly and evenly flared and the second, having several baluster turns between breech and muzzle, very much like a cannon barrel. As in their larger counterparts, these blunderbuss pistols were often fitted with spring bayonets, which sprang out on retracting the trigger-guard or operating a catch on the top or side of the weapon.

John Waters, who first patented the spring bayonet, produced blunderbuss pistols of the first type, while Philip Bond of Cornhill favoured the second, his pistols being of large dimensions, with slabsided butts.

Joseph Heylin was another well-known maker who specialized in these very handsome pistols.

Double-Barrelled Pistols

A double-barrelled, 'over-and-under' flintlock pistol has already been described.

However, double-barrelled flintlock pistols, which are of the 'side-by-side' variety, are also found, such pistols being fitted with two locks, one on each side of the weapon.

Yet another variety of double-barrelled pistol consists of 'over-and-under' barrels, having locks on either side of the frame. Joseph and Durs Egg both made exquisite examples of this type of gun, using external mainsprings.

Three-Barrelled Pistols

These, too, were not uncommon, and were operated on the 'tap' principle, with a different position for each barrel. The barrel arrangement consisted of two barrels lying side by side with the third situated centrally below.

Segalas Pistols

Another pistol worthy of mention is a flintlock pistol of small dimensions know as a 'Segalas' pistol, sometimes spelt 'Seglas'. This pistol is usually of all-metal construction, with an engraved, bag-shaped butt, and was double or even quadruple cannon-barrelled. These weapons were of Belgian origin.

Round-Frame Pistols

A further variety of pistol will occasionally be encountered. This is a flintlock or percussion boxlock pocket pistol, which has a round frame instead of the more usual square frame. Such pistols are most attractive, and are sometimes to be found with fluted barrels.

Eprouvette

This unusually shaped item was used in order to test the strength of black powder. It has a walnut butt and brass frame, with the maker's name engraved upon it in the manner of the normal pocket pistol. However, instead of a barrel, a graduated disc is fitted, from which readings of powder strength can be obtained.

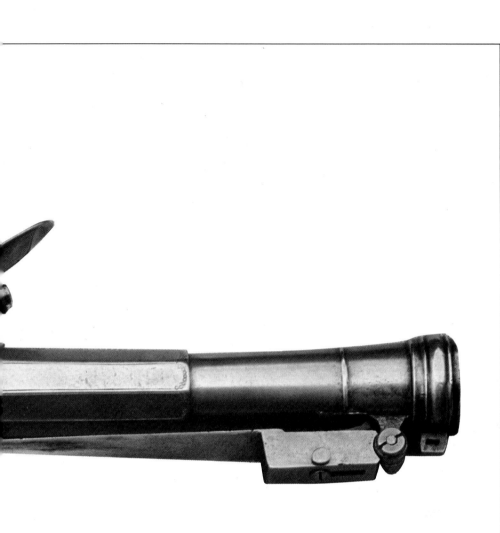

Blunderbuss pistol by the famous gunmaker Henry Nock. Note the spring bayonet

Colt Revolvers

Colt Roots revolver. This weapon, produced in 1855, was named after Elisha King Root, who was Colt's factory superintendent. It had a plain or fluted cylinder, according to preference, and had no trigger-guard, being fitted instead with a 'sheath' trigger. It was made in 0.28 and 0.31 inch calibres.

Police Model. This 0.36 inch calibre revolver of 1862 has a fluted cylinder. It can still be found today in very crisp condition, with much original finish.

Round-barrelled Colt Navy. Mention has been made of both the Colt Army and Navy models, but in 1861 a streamlined version of the Navy was produced, looking very much like the Army model but without the rebated cylinder, and being of Navy calibre – 0.36 inch. This is the round-barrelled Colt Navy, and is a relatively rare item.

Colt Dragoon. Following on from the success of the Walker Colt in 1847, a 0.44 inch calibre hand 'cannon' which weighed more than $4\frac{1}{2}$ lb, Samuel Colt produced three models of his Colt Dragoon revolvers, identified by the shape of the trigger-guard and the cylinder-bolt recesses. Still very heavy and unwieldy round-barrelled weapons, they had a calibre of 0.44 inch, with a $7\frac{1}{2}$-inch or 8-inch barrel.

Colt Army revolver

Remington Revolver

Manufactured by Eliphalet Remington at his factory in Ilion, New York, this percussion revolver was similar in many respects to the Colt, but had a 'closed' frame, which made it more robust and less likely to be damaged when dropped. Patented in 1858, it was issued mainly in 0.36 inch and 0.44 inch calibres, and was six-shot, with five groove rifling. Like the Colt, it was used extensively by both sides during the American Civil War.

Adams Revolver

This revolver was the main competitor in England to the Colt Navy revolver. Colt's weapons were single action and required to be cocked each time before firing. The Adams double-action mechanism allowed a single trigger pull to cock and fire the weapon in one movement. It is known that tremendous controversy raged between the protagonists of each revolver, those favouring the Adams asserting that it was faster firing and of a larger calibre than the Colt and therefore had more 'stopping' power. On the other hand, the heavier trigger pull of the Adams tended to force that revolver off target, whereas the single action of the Colt permitted more accurate aiming.

Having handled both weapons, it is self-evident that the Adams in its original form was useless from the point of view of accuracy, due to the considerable pressure necessary to operate the

trigger and fire the weapon. Its safety mechanism was also extremely dangerous. The hammer, after being slightly cocked, is allowed to rest on the safety catch, and any sudden jolt could cause it to jump off its safety and detonate a charge in the cylinder. This was a tremendous hazard, especially to someone on horseback. Consequently the weapon was crying out for its subsequent modification in 1854, and again in 1856, when, in its final form, as the Beaumont Adams revolver, it became eminently suited to its role as the favoured personal sidearm of the British Army officer.

Webley Revolver

This Birmingham firm produced several models of percussion revolver. Their weapons were five-shot and were manufactured in three models, the first with detachable ramrod, the second with attached ramrod and the third with the more robust and dependable Kerr-type rammer, used also on the Beaumont Adams revolver. The three models were characterized by an elongated hammer spur, and were consequently known as 'Longspur' revolvers.

Later, a fourth model was produced, which incorporated a wedge similar to the Colt's and was therefore known as the Webley 'Wedgeframe'.

A variant is the Webley Bentley revolver, in which the safety involves a catch on the hammer nose.

Tranter Revolver

William Tranter was a Birmingham gunsmith who produced Adams revolvers under licence. However, Tranter developed a unique double-trigger mechanism which he himself patented. The lower trigger cocked the weapon, which was then fired by pulling the upper trigger. Pulling both triggers together allowed the revolver to be used 'double-action'.

His final percussion revolver had a single trigger, incorporating a small spur at the rear, which disengaged the sear when the trigger was pulled, so allowing the hammer to fall.

Matchlock

I have never had a matchlock in my collection of antique firearms. Matchlock pistols of Japanese origin, with highly polished stocks and brass springs and furniture, do exist, but were probably intended only as toys, as the matchlock mechanism does not really lend itself to hand-held operation. The direction of travel of the serpen-

Percussion Jaeger rifle by Lindenschmit

Matchlock

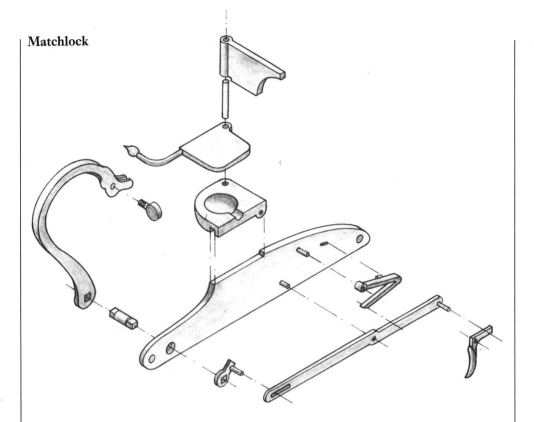

tine can be useful in determining the country of origin of matchlocks. In Japanese versions, which are very distinctive, the serpentine moves forward towards the pan when the trigger is pressed, and the same is true of Indian matchlocks, or Toradors. In European matchlocks, however, the direction of travel is backwards, towards the shooter.

Wheel-lock

I regret to say that no wheel-lock as yet adorns the walls of my happy home, and probably no one else's either, since these valuable items belong in bank vaults or safety-deposit boxes.

Wheel-locks date from the 16th century until the third quarter of the 17th century, when flint finally supplanted iron pyrites in the new French locks of the day.

There are two principal types. The first is heavily inlaid with ivory and has a large ball pommel. These pistols often have the town mark of Augsburg or Nuremberg on the barrel, with the maker's mark impressed on the lockplate. Such weapons were widely copied in Victorian times and have now acquired an appropriately aged appearance. It therefore behoves the collector to tread warily.

The second variety has a longer barrel, some-

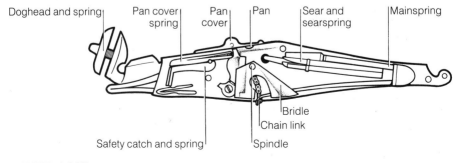

Doghead and spring | Pan cover spring | Pan cover | Pan | Sear and searspring | Mainspring

Bridle
Chain link
Safety catch and spring | Spindle

WHEEL-LOCK

times faceted, and has much more graceful lines, being frequently of Dutch origin and of a type often used during the English Civil War. It is this latter version which I prefer and would dearly love to possess, but this is likely to remain a pipe dream for myself as well as most other collectors.

French Pistols
This account would be incomplete without mentioning these much underrated weapons. They are frequently to be found at arms fairs, generally set up in fitted French-style cases, in which the pistols and accessories, usually of the highest quality, are accurately enclosed in contoured recesses.

The pistols are most often of the percussion target variety, having pronounced angular grips with elaborately carved stocks. The barrels are blued, with much gold inlay, and the lockplates are also blued and gilded. These cases look quite magnificent and, considering their quality and craftsmanship, do not as yet command the high prices which they deserve.

Enfield Rifle
This rifle was adopted by the British Army in 1853. It had a 39-inch barrel, with three barrel bands, and was rifled with three grooves. The weapon fired a conical bullet of 0.577 inch calibre, and is much favoured by black-powder shooters to this day.

Whitworth Rifle
Another British weapon, this gun was manufactured in Manchester by Sir Joseph Whitworth. It incorporated hexagonal rifling. This rifle was precision made to the highest standards, and was reckoned to be more accurate than the Enfield.

The Confederate States showed interest in purchasing the gun during the American Civil War.

Kentucky Rifle
Sometimes known as the Pennsylvanian rifle, this weapon was developed from the Jaeger rifle of the early German settlers. Its lines were very graceful, the stock being beautifully shaped and of striped maple, often inlaid with brass or silver, and incorporating a patch box. The weapons were used even in the percussion era, and it is not uncommon to find flintlocks converted to percussion. Kentucky rifles are both valuable and very rare, and are said to have been a decisive factor in the defeat of the British Army at the Battle of New Orleans in 1812.

Tower Pistols
In the chapter discussing the many variations of this type of pistol, some examples are not represented. These are:
1. Royal Horse Guards pistol. This weapon has a single ramrod pipe, a flat lockplate and cock, a 10-inch barrel, a butt-cap with long side tangs and a grotesque mask.
2. A William IV Dragoon pistol, with bolted lock, swivel ramrod, rounded butt-cap and 9-inch barrel.
3. A William IV Sea-service pistol with swivel ramrod, belt hook and 9-inch barrel.
4. A plain pistol without butt-cap, incorporating Nock's screwless lock, with 9-inch barrel.
5. Lancer's pistol. Pattern 1842, with 9-inch barrel.

Baker Rifle
Selected in 1800 to arm the Rifle Regiment, this flintlock rifle had a 30-inch barrel, and a calibre of 0.615 inch. It had seven-groove rifling and used a sword bayonet. The stock was relatively straight, and incorporated a brass patch box. The trigger-guard was also of brass, and was extended at the rear as a grip for the last three fingers of the right hand.

Duck's Foot Pistol
This weapon is essentially an ordinary boxlock pistol, with slabsided butt and four barrels, which radiate outwards like the fingers of an outstretched hand. Many were made by Forth of York and incorporate a belt hook. These strange weapons were thought to be ideal for use at sea, in case it should be necessary for the officers to defend themselves against mutinous sailors. Today, many more of these guns are available than were originally made, and I personally would think very carefully indeed before purchasing one.

Spanish Pistols
These weapons have miquelet locks with an external mainspring that presses against the heel of the cock. The frizzen is deeply grooved and the flint jaws are enormous, with a ring-shaped top-jaw screw. These pistols have ball butts and a spur on the trigger-guard.

Cossack Pistols
These pistols also have miquelet locks and an ivory ball butt. With their long barrels and silver barrel bands, they have a very strange and distinctive appearance.

Classification and Development
of Antique Firearms

Antique firearms can be classified in many different ways. The first and most obvious distinction is between pistols and long arms, the latter having a pronounced shoulder stock and a length of at least 2 feet 6 inches, and which may be smooth bored or rifled.

Pistols may be classified according to lock type, i.e., flint, percussion, etc., but are most commonly classified according to size, pocket size being up to eight inches in length, overcoat size eight to eleven inches, coach pistols thirteen to fifteen inches, and holster pistols over sixteen inches in length. Such a classification is, of course, entirely arbitrary, and overlap between classes may occur.

Duelling pistols are sixteen to eighteen inches in length, but tend to be classified rather by their style and the possession of certain characteristic features.

Pistols may be multiple, single or double barrelled, and the double barrels may be either 'side by side', or 'over and under', depending on their relationship to one another. A further type of pistol is known as a belt pistol, on account of its belt hook.

Revolvers, including both pepperboxes and transition revolvers, represent further types of handgun.

Early flintlock pistols were long-barrelled weapons, with fishtail butts, and had butt-caps with long side tangs. They were often silver mounted, full-stocked to the muzzle, and had rounded locks and cocks, the locks being banana shaped in outline. Triggers had a backward curl at the lower end. These early pistols had no bridle, either to the tumbler or frizzen, but this was in common usage after the first quarter of the 18th century, and by 1740 was virtually a standard feature.

As the 18th century progressed, barrels became progressively shorter, locks less banana shaped, and were either of rounded or flattened form. By about 1770, side tangs had virtually disappeared. The barrels, up till this date, were secured to the stock by pins.

Around 1750, a very elegant pistol with a ball butt and grotesque mask appeared. This type of pistol often had elaborate escutcheons and side-plates, but with a barrel only nine inches in length. Triggers were less curved, and the backward curl became solid rather than hollow.

The Queen Anne pistol had made its appearance in the early part of the century, being of boxlock construction, but with a side hammer.

The weapon had a cannon barrel of the 'screw-off' variety and a characteristic grotesque mask butt-cap with a serpentine sideplate. A variant had a side lock instead of the usual lock. Much later in the century another and less elaborate type of cannon-barrelled pistol appeared that had a slab-sided butt with silver wire inlay, but with a central swung cock. Early Queen Anne pistols were often marked 'Londini', and had silver wire inlay, which tended to disappear towards the middle part of the century.

By the end of the 18th century, stocks had lost their butt-caps and sideplates, and were of hockey-stick shape, often finely chequered. Half-stock weapons were beginning to appear. Locks had become flat in section and had refinements such as roller frizzens and rainproof pans. Triggers lost their backward curl, becoming narrower and straighter. The barrels were secured to the stock by means of flat wedges.

Escutcheons had now become vestigial plates, and a false breech, for ease in dismantling, came into vogue. The lock was secured by one or two 'sidenails', which fitted into a 'cup' recess. Cocks, rounded in section during the first half of the century, became more flattened, while trigger-guard finials, husk shaped until about 1750, became acorn shaped and finally pineapple shaped.

In the first quarter of the 19th century, the boxlock flintlock pistol was developed and, when combined with a folding trigger, was ideal for slipping into the pocket for personal protection. The cock in such pistols was known as the 'throat-hole' or 'ring-neck' variety. Ladies could use smaller versions, known as muff pistols.

Scottish pistols had their own particular style. Of all-metal construction, the 17th-century weapons had fishtail butts and snaphaunce locks. In the late 17th century, the heart-shaped butt developed. After about 1725, the pistols had scroll or ramshorn butts. At about the same time, the lobe-butted pistol became popular. In the third quarter of the century the ramshorn butt was produced in a somewhat shortened version. Two further types of Scottish pistol – both military versions – were manufactured in Birmingham, one by Isaac Bisell and the other by John Waters.

Percussion locks began to appear in the second quarter of the 19th century. By 1850, the pepperbox had made its appearance, and, shortly afterwards, the percussion revolver began to dominate the firearms industry.

Dismantling Antique Firearms

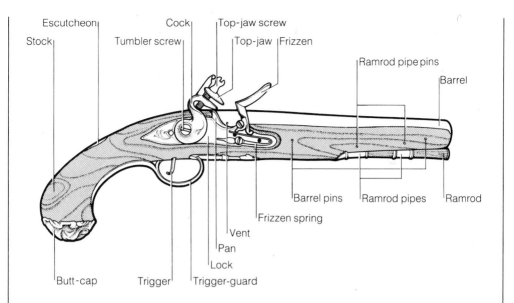

FLINTLOCK PISTOL

Escutcheon — Cock — Top-jaw screw
Stock — Tumbler screw — Top-jaw — Frizzen
Ramrod pipe pins
Barrel
Barrel pins — Ramrod pipes — Ramrod
Frizzen spring
Vent
Pan
Lock
Butt-cap — Trigger — Trigger-guard

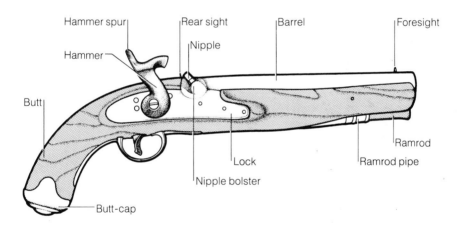

PERCUSSION PISTOL

Hammer spur — Rear sight — Barrel — Foresight
Nipple
Hammer
Butt
Ramrod
Lock — Ramrod pipe
Nipple bolster
Butt-cap

Before embarking on this chapter, it is worth mentioning that it is encumbent on every collector of antique firearms to take care of the weapons in his collection, in order to preserve them for future generations. Just as Florence Nightingale stated that the most important tenet of the nursing profession was that they should never cause harm to any of their patients, the gun collector is in an analogous situation in that, whatever he may do to the guns in his collection, he should never inflict any damage upon them.

Sidelock Flintlocks

It will be seen that this type of lock is secured by two large screws passing right through the stock from the opposite side. These screws, often referred to as sidenails, are usually removed without much difficulty. Nevertheless it is important to ensure that a tight-fitting screwdriver is used, the blade of which penetrates to the bottom of the screw slot. The gun should be firmly supported, and it is preferable to place the thumb and fore-finger of the opposite hand on either side

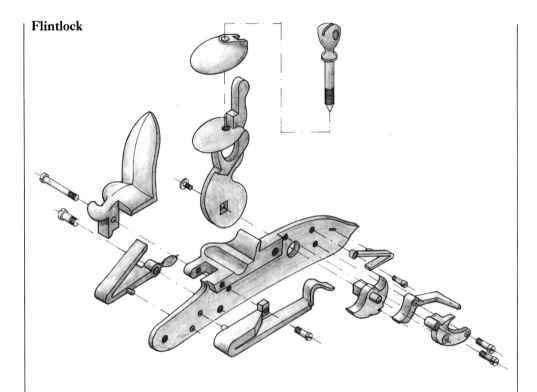

of the blade in the initial stages in order to prevent the screwdriver slipping off and perhaps damaging the stock.

The cock is then placed in the half-cock position, and the lock is eased out by lateral pressure on the cock itself. If the lock is a tight fit, as is often the case in high-quality weapons, the sidenails should be replaced, and given one or two turns only. Firm pressure, or light tapping, on the screw heads will then release the lock. Undue force may cause a slip of wood to break off, so great care should be taken with a tight lock.

Some locks of high quality are secured by a single screw at the front, the tail of the lock engaging in a tiny catch at the rear of the lock recess.

The lock is then placed on full cock, and release oil applied to all internal screws. Remove the mainspring-retaining screw, if present. The hand vice is then applied to the mainspring, after first fitting the jaw protectors. This is then tightened, but only to the point to which it is already compressed, since overtightening will cause the spring to fracture. Pressure on the tail of the sear will then free the cock, and the mainspring can be lifted out.

The tumbler screw is now removed and the cock eased off the tumbler. If this is unsuccessful, brass wedges may be tapped gently between the lockplate and the cock on either side, and the cock can then be removed. The top-jaw screw is extracted after the liberal application of release oil. Next, the sear spring retaining screw is partially loosened, and the sear spring prised out of the lockplate into which it is slotted by means of a penknife blade. The sear pivot screw, and the sear itself, are then removed. The second bridle screw is then extracted, freeing first the bridle and, finally, the tumbler itself.

The frizzen is placed in the position giving maximum compression of the frizzen spring. The clamp is then applied and the retaining screw extracted. The frizzen is closed and the frizzen spring lifted out. Finally the frizzen retaining screw is removed, allowing the frizzen itself to slip out of its bridle.

Turning to the weapon itself, the sideplate is removed when the two sidenails are extracted. The barrel tang screw is then removed, followed by the barrel pins. These should be tapped out very carefully, using a pin punch of the correct size and a light hammer, supporting the gun on wooden blocks, preferably covered with hard rubber. A careless attempt to remove these pins will result in the punch slipping off the head of the pin and cutting its own hole in the stock. If barrel wedges are used, these should be tapped out using the blade of a screwdriver, but only sufficiently to clear the barrel loops into which they are slotted, each wedge being secured permanently to the stock by means of a small pin passing through its centre; on no account should these be removed.

The barrel can now be lifted out of the stock. No attempt should be made to remove ramrod pipes, nor should butt-caps be disturbed. The latter are usually well secured by their retaining screw, which is often difficult to remove anyway, and the screw head will probably be damaged in the process. The trigger-guard, where secured by screws, may then be removed. However, if, as is often the case, they are held in position by means of pins, it is often better to leave them undisturbed, since these pins are frequently a very tight fit in the stock, and attempted removal will have no real benefit and in fact may simply result in permanent damage. Most repair work, such as removal of pitting, can be carried out with the guard *in situ*. It is seldom necessary to remove the trigger, but this can easily be done by tapping out the retaining pin. It is better to work from the opposite side to the lock recess, because this pin is usually a very tight fit, and might take a piece of stock with it if tapped from the inside.

A feature of duelling pistols is the detent, which is a small strip of metal attached to the tumbler, the function of which is to prevent the sear, when the trigger is pressed, catching in the half-cock bent. It was a refinement used in weapons which had a 'set' or 'hair' trigger.

A variation found in some flintlock pistols is the apparent absence of a barrel tang screw. In these, generally very early pistols, the barrel tang is secured by a long screw inserted through the stock and into the tang from below, the screw head being concealed by the trigger-guard.

Once stripped, the lock parts usually benefit from cleaning with fine wire wool, although occasionally it may be necessary to use wet and dry sandpaper first, in order to remove any rust.

All the screw threads should be cleaned out by pressing a piece of tissue or cottonwool soaked in oil against the thread with the thumbnail while using a screwdriver in the other hand to 'unscrew' it. This effectively removes all dirt and old oil, and the process should be repeated with a dry tissue. All the female threads in the lockplate are cleaned out, using cottonwool rolled round the point of a rat-tail file, which is then 'screwed' into the hole, and out again, and repeated with fresh cottonwool until no more dirt appears on the wool.

All female threads are then oiled, and the lock reassembled in reverse order.

When refitting the sear spring, its retaining screw should be screwed in as far as possible. Pressure on the rear of the spring will cause it to locate in its tiny recess, and the screw can then be fully driven home.

When replacing the mainspring, it is necessary to make sure that its locating peg is properly seated in its recess.

Set trigger

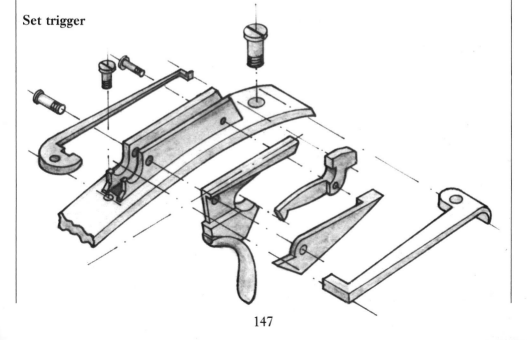

147

Finally the mainspring and all moving parts should be lightly oiled.

The barrel should be checked for obstructions. This is easily done by means of a metal rod or piece of dowelling, measuring the distance it travels down the barrel and comparing this to the distance from the muzzle to the breech on the outside of the barrel. The bore is then oiled. When replacing the barrel pins, great care should be taken that these travel down the holes designed for them, rather than creating new ones.

If there is no original finish on the metal parts of the gun, these usually benefit from being burnished with fine wire wool. Brasswork should be polished using proprietary polishes but, if badly tarnished, this is best achieved with wire wool soaked in polish, the job being completed by further application of polish in the usual way, finishing off with a soft cloth.

Silver furniture is best treated with silver polish on a soft cloth, and wire wool should not be used. Badly tarnished silver can be treated with silver dip.

Percussion Sidelocks

These may be dealt with in precisely the same manner as flintlock weapons. If the nipple is undamaged, then no attempt need be made to remove it. This is a difficult procedure in any case, as the combination of dirt and rust accumulating between the threads can take many weeks of immersion in release oil to permit them to be unscrewed.

Percussion weapons often had a hook breech, the barrel tang being a separate piece. Removal of the barrel in these weapons is carried out by, firstly, putting the weapon on half cock, then removing the barrel wedges and lifting the muzzle

upwards, causing the hook to disengage from the recess into which it is fitted.

Percussion Back-Action Lock

In this type of lock, the mainspring acts from the rear, pulling up on the tumbler by means of a short stirrup. The sear spring may be either separate or an extension of the mainspring.

Many percussion locks have a tiny linkage, similar to the one described above, which joins the tumbler to the mainspring, and makes for a smoother-acting lock.

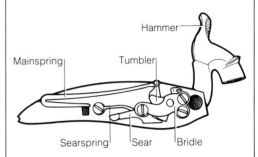

PERCUSSION BACK-ACTION LOCK

Boxlock Flintlock

This is the commonest type of lock encountered. The method of dismantling is as follows:

Unscrew the turn-off barrel. Remove the frizzen spring screw, then the frizzen spring. Remove the frizzen retaining screw and the frizzen itself.

Turn out the two screws attaching the butt. Remove butt. Unscrew the two screws holding the top strap to the frame. The top strap should then be pushed as far up the cock as it will travel, in order to permit the hand vice to be used.

Put the gun at full cock, thus compressing the mainspring to its full extent. Place the hand-vice on the mainspring, as near to the upper end as possible, the lower jaw round the backstrap, not forgetting to protect the backstrap with insulating tape, and using the vice jaw covers.

Uncock the pistol. Turn out cock screw. Remove cock. Remove mainspring. Now tap out the pin holding the trigger in place and remove the trigger. Push out the trigger spring by slipping the blade of a small screwdriver behind it and pushing forwards, when its locating pin will be disengaged. Remove the screw securing the rear of the trigger-guard. If the guard is then rotated, the front end of the trigger-guard will disengage from its seating.

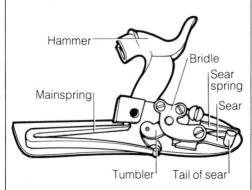

PERCUSSION SIDE LOCK

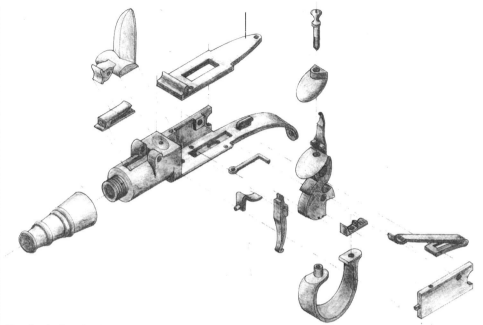

Boxlock flintlock

The safety catch, often a feature of the top strap, can be disassembled if need be by unscrewing the little screw securing its spring and removing the spring. A tiny pin is then tapped out to allow the safety catch to be removed.

Some flintlock pistols have a different form of frizzen spring from the V-shaped external one described above. This, too, is V-shaped, but instead of being fitted externally to the frizzen it is sunk into a recess in the breech and only its top surface is visible. This type of frizzen spring can be held down by thumb pressure while the frizzen screw is removed.

Boxlock Percussion Pistol with Sidehammer
Some boxlock pistols have a sidehammer instead of the normal centre-swung hammer. However, dismantling these does not really present any problem.

The top plate is unscrewed, the butt detached and the mainspring compressed. The hammer is then removed from the tumbler. The opposite side of the boxlock frame is detachable, and is removed by unscrewing a countersunk screw which lies underneath, at the side of the trigger-guard, and pulling the side backwards to disengage its locating stud. The tumbler and mainspring are then removed, the trigger-pin tapped

out, and the trigger and trigger spring extracted. The trigger-guard can be removed in the usual way.

Double-Barrelled Pistols
When a pistol has two mainsprings, these have to be individually compressed before the single hammer screw can be removed. This can be achieved by the use of two hand vices, or by constructing a fixed clamp of the precise width of the compressed mainspring, measuring from the front of the backstrap. The first hammer is then cocked and the clamp slipped on to the compressed spring. The hand vice is then applied to the second hammer and, after the triggers have been pressed to free the hammers, the hammer screw can then be removed.

Queen Anne Flintlock Pistol
The mechanism of this pistol is similar to that of a percussion sidehammer pistol, except that when the stock is removed the tumbler is seen to be pivoted between two bearings – on the one side the frame through which its squared end projects, to receive the cock, and on the other a steel plate fixed to the base of the pistol by a large screw. This plate has to be removed in order to extract the tumbler.

Queen Anne pistols often have a safety catch, operated by pushing the trigger-guard forward, moving a metal slide against spring pressure, and this mechanism should be studied carefully before dismantling.

Bar Hammer Pepperbox

First remove the central screw between the barrels and draw off the barrel block. The two woodscrews attaching the stock are then removed, and the butt is carefully drawn off the top and bottom straps. The two screws securing the top strap are next extracted, and the top strap is pushed along the bar hammer as far as possible. The bar hammer is then raised in order to compress the V-shaped mainspring, which is then held in the hand-vice. The hammer screw and the bar hammer itself, along with its somewhat complicated mechanism, are now extracted.

The pawl spring and its retaining screw are next extracted. The mainspring is lifted out. The sideplate is removed by extracting the screw at the side of the trigger-guard. The pawl screw and the pawl itself, which advances the barrel block when the trigger is pulled, are then removed. The trigger-spring, with its retaining screw, can now be removed, exposing the rear screw of the trigger-guard. If this is now extracted, the trigger-guard can be disengaged from its front attach-

BAR HAMMER PEPPERBOX

ment. Finally, the trigger pivot screw and the trigger itself are both removed.

Cooper Pepperbox

This is essentially similar to the bar hammer pepperbox, except that there is a ring trigger rather than the conventional type, and the hammer operates from below. The mainspring in this type of pepperbox is a curved piece of spring steel, rather than the V-shaped spring of the pepperbox mechanism described above. The two-piece grip has a bag-shaped outline.

Cooper pepperbox

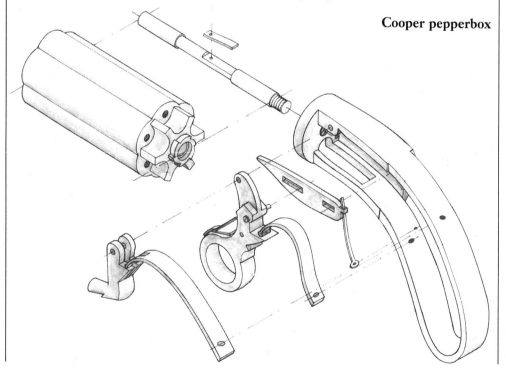

Colt Navy revolver

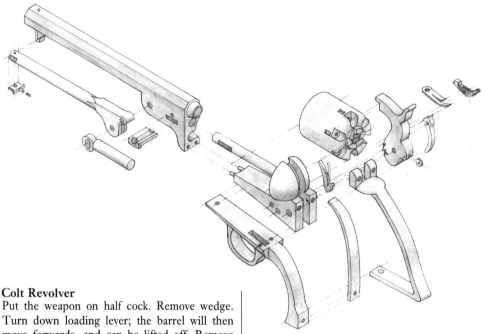

Colt Revolver

Put the weapon on half cock. Remove wedge. Turn down loading lever; the barrel will then move forwards, and can be lifted off. Remove cylinder. Remove butt by extracting a single screw from the bottom strap and two screws near the hammer. Disengage the mainspring by pressing to one side. Remove trigger-guard – three screws. Remove the screw retaining the combined cylinder bolt/trigger spring and remove the spring.

Remove cylinder-bolt screw and cylinder bolt. Remove trigger screw and trigger. Finally, remove hammer screw and hammer, taking care to observe how the pawl is attached to it by a peg and slots into its own channel.

Adams Revolver

Pull out cylinder pin and remove cylinder by pushing it out to the right. When replacing the cylinder, this must be done in reverse. Remove the wood screw securing the butt to the backstrap and the screw passing through the top strap into the butt-supporting plate. This little plate has another screw which need not be removed. Unscrew the two trigger-guard screws and re-move the guard with the concealed trigger-spring. Observe the position of this spring for reassembly. Remove trigger screw and trigger with its pawl and sear. Remove safety catch with its retaining screw. Finally, remove hammer screw and lift off hammer whilst compressing mainspring – thumb pressure may be sufficient. The mainspring can then be lifted off.

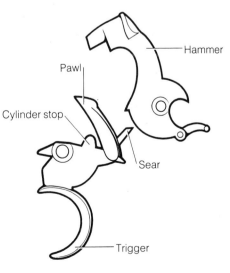

ADAMS DOUBLE ACTION

151

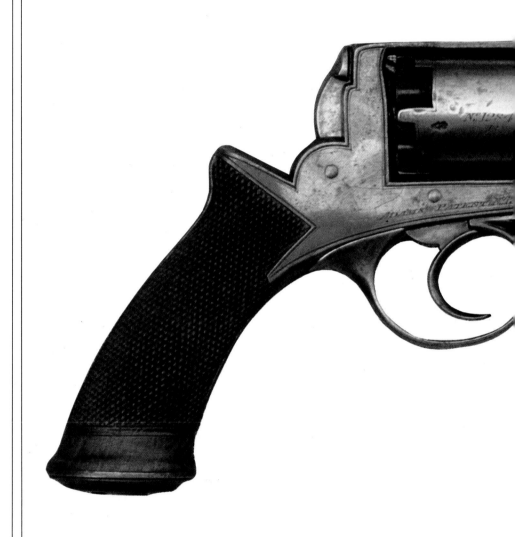

Adams percussion revolver, Improved Frame

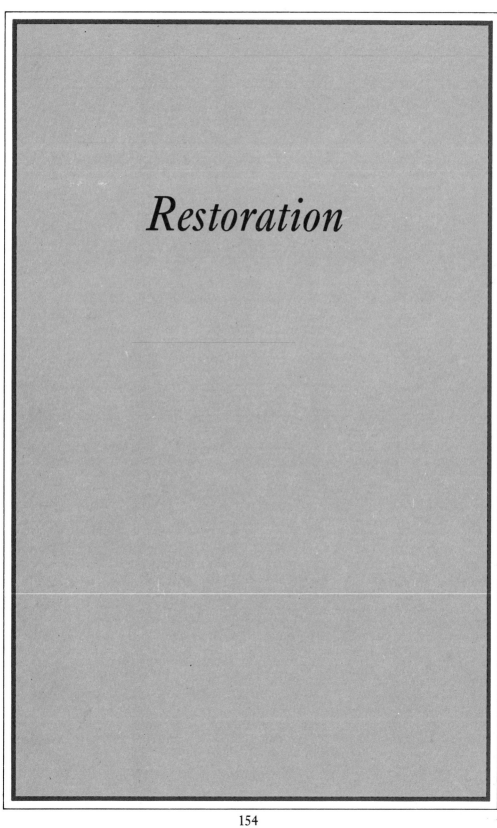

Restoration

I make no apology for beginning this chapter as I did the last, with a caveat. The restoration of antique firearms is not an easy task yet, on the other hand, it can be mastered by anyone who is prepared to spend a disproportionate amount of time, and a great deal of effort, in order to achieve it. The great watchword of the restorer of antique weapons is patience. Every job must be carefully assessed before embarking upon it, and on no account should it be tackled before this has been done.

It may be that a particular task can be approached in various ways, and the apprentice restorer should turn the problem over and over in his mind until the most appropriate solution at last becomes clear to him. In my own case, this can take several hours of thoughtful consideration of a particular problem.

Antique firearms are, after all, very valuable items, and faulty or slipshod work by the restorer may ruin the piece for ever. He must be a perfectionist, never satisfied with his efforts, always seeking to improve upon his techniques as well as upon the end result of his labours.

Before getting down to the practicalities of restoration work, it is important that mention should be made both of the tools which the restorer will require and the workshop in which his miracles will be performed.

When I myself first began to immerse myself in the mysteries of antique gun restoration, being a general medical practitioner I knew virtually nothing whatsoever about engineering or woodwork. Perhaps this may give some heart to those readers who feel a certain amount of nervousness about the mechanics of restoration. Books, of course, were available on restoration procedures, but I felt that they were not particularly suited to amateurs like myself and, in any case, did not describe at all some of the essential techniques of gunsmithing. In fact, most of my own techniques have been discovered in what might be called the hard way, by trial and error, by uncovering evidence of inferior restoration and having to put matters right, and the reader will find exactly the same. He will inevitably make some mistakes at first, but as he begins to gain confidence will gradually acquire proficiency in the various techniques involved in the art of the gunsmith, which will continue to improve with the passage of time.

There are many guns available today that are in need of restoration, and the prices are correspondingly lower, so that it is still quite possible to build up a collection of antique firearms from such pieces and at the same time have the satisfaction of restoring them to something approaching their former glory.

While it is highly desirable that the restorer has a separate workshop in which to carry on the practice of his art, this is not always possible. In my own case, I was obliged to convert a corner of my garage. Ideally, the workroom should be fairly compact but well lit, ventilated and heated. A carpet covering over the concrete floor is a considerable benefit in wintertime.

A *bench* of some kind is essential. To this is secured an *engineer's vice*, with 3-inch or 4-inch jaws. In order to prevent damage to gun stocks, barrels and other gun parts, it is essential to make vice *jaw covers*. These can be easily constructed from an appropriate length of ¾-inch copper piping, using metal snips to cut the pipe, which can then be hammered flat on an anvil and bent to shape in the vice. The edges are smoothed using a file and wet and dry sandpaper. Copper covers will cause the least damage to metal parts, especially if these are delicate, as with small screws.

A whole set of *screwdrivers* of different lengths and sizes must be obtained. These should be kept purely for restoration work, and strictly not used for the car or other household jobs. *Pliers* are needed, of both the normal and long-nosed variety. *Wrenches*, for removing barrels, will be required. A *blowlamp* will be needed. A *hand vice*, and a set of jaw protectors, must be obtained. *Files*, of various shapes and sizes, are also essential, and a set of fine Swiss files should be purchased. A shaped *rasp* is required for stock repair work. A light (4 oz) *ball pein hammer*, with a heavier one for larger jobs, is necessary. Various *pin punches* will be needed, and a large *hacksaw*, as well as a Junior hacksaw, must be found. *File card* is very useful for cleaning files. A *hand drill* and a set of twist drills will also be needed. A *centre punch*, a *scriber* and a 12-inch *metal ruler* are all essential. An *electric drill* can help occasionally, and sometimes a *bench drill*, although these are not absolutely essential. A *lathe* is also not essential, but can save both time and expense in many jobs. *Taps and dies* are necessary for screw cutting. Lastly, a stock of walnut, and perhaps some ebony, is indispensable to the restorer, and one must use one's ingenuity in order to obtain these, possibly from a sympathetic local gunsmith or antique dealer.

STOCK REPAIR

Fore-end. In repairing the fore-end of a stock, the first essential is to cut off the shattered wood. Never cut this perpendicular to the stock as the repair will be both weak and obvious. The cut should be made at an angle, using a Junior hacksaw blade. This is best done by mounting the stock firmly in the vice, with a narrow strip of wood on either side to protect it. Hold a flat piece of metal against it to ensure that the cut is absolutely straight. If not, it should be sanded with medium-grade sandpaper wrapped around a flat file or wooden strip. Great care should be taken not to round off the edges, as it is essential that these remain crisp and sharp. A piece of walnut of matching grain is found, and this is cut at an angle corresponding to that already cut in the stock. If this angle is incorrectly cut, it can be adjusted using the sander. The piece of walnut used should be wider, longer and deeper than necessary, to allow for adjustment in fitting.

The new fore-end should be roughly shaped by marking the outline of the stock contours onto the proximal end, and the barrel recess should also be cut out by placing it in the vice, making saw cuts on either side in a V shape and finishing off roughly with a round rasp and medium sandpaper.

It is of vital importance that the stock recess and the barrel are accurately fitted to one another. Stocks were meticulously fitted by 18th-century gunsmiths, and a less than perfect fit will make the repair more obtrusive to critical inspection.

However, the exterior of the new fore-end need only be an approximate fit at this early stage, final and more accurate fitting being much easier after the fore-end has been glued in position. The fore-end can now be shortened to the desired length – usually just short of the muzzle.

Next, using medium sandpaper wrapped around a round file or piece of wood dowelling, the stock recess is deepened and widened until the new fore-end and barrel are a perfect fit, and the joint between the stock and the new fore-end is closed. The fore-end should be repeatedly offered into position, with the barrel taped to the stock, to ensure that an excess of wood is not removed.

The last stages should be carried out using only fine sandpaper, and great care should be taken that the recess is neither wider nor deeper than necessary, as such a result will be immediately obvious.

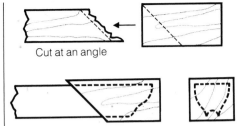

Cut at an angle

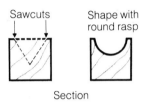

Roughly shape new fore-end after marking outline

Sawcuts   Shape with round rasp

Section

Making barrel recess

Using resin glue to coat the surfaces to be joined, the two ends are now apposed. Excess glue is then removed, especially from the barrel recess. The barrel is placed *in situ*, inserting a piece of tissue paper first, to cover the join. It is then tightly bound to the stock and fore-end with string and placed upright, so that its weight compresses the fore-end. The presence of tissue prevents the barrel from adhering to the repair, and it can be easily scraped away afterwards.

The repair should be left in a warm atmosphere for forty-eight hours. After this time, the restorer may proceed to finish off the exterior. The new fore-end should now be shaped to the correct contour, using medium sandpaper wrapped around a $\frac{1}{2}$-inch file, taking great care not to mark the undamaged stock.

The ramrod groove is then filed into it, using a round file and finishing off with sandpaper.

After using medium sandpaper, fine sandpaper can then be applied, to give a satin-smooth finish. As the human eye is capable of detecting even the slightest deviation from normal, it is imperative that the new fore-end perfectly matches the rest of the stock in height as well as contour.

However, the job is still not complete because, if stain were to be applied at this stage to the new wood, it would cause the grain to rise, so that all new wood must be 'whiskered'. To do this, moisten the new fore-end with the finger dipped in water. When the wood is dry, and a finger run over its surface, it will be found that the grain has risen. This should be very lightly sanded with fine sandpaper, and the process repeated three or four times until the stage is reached when moistening produces no further rise in grain.

The wood is then ready for staining.

A splice carried out in this manner can seldom entirely escape detection, as the tell-tale join is visible despite staining, yet it is infinitely preferable to the broken stock which existed before.

Never leave any sharp edges to the new wood – look at the edges of the undamaged stock and lightly sandpaper the edges of the new fore-end so that they have similarly worn edges and corners.

Walnut stain should now be applied to the new wood only and allowed to dry for twenty-four hours. After this time, if the colour is not a good match, it can be stained again, and this process can be repeated as often as necessary. The walnut stain may be darkened by mixing with a tiny amount of black shoe-leather dye. Always test the resulting colour on another piece of wood, in case the shade is too dark.

The great benefit of using epoxy resin is that it is not only an excellent adhesive, it also acts as a grain filler, and readily takes up stain.

Whilst replacement of the fore-end, especially if this is a long section, is the most difficult of stock repairs, as the angled edges tend to slide off whilst apposition is being attempted, all wood damage is treated in a similar way, generally by filing the edges straight and splicing in a piece of walnut of slightly larger size than necessary, roughly shaped before fitting. It is then firmly fixed in position, either by using a clamp or, quite effectively, using sticky tape. After twenty-four to forty-eight hours, the more accurate shaping with sandpaper begins, and finishing is carried out in the usual way, with fine sandpaper and staining.

Always ensure that the grain of the new walnut runs in exactly the same direction as that of the undamaged stock, otherwise the repair will be immediately obvious.

With a partial fore-end repair, once the edges have been filed straight, a small block of walnut can be offered into position, as shown in the diagram (overleaf). Subsequent rough shaping is then easier.

Where the existing stock is highly polished, it is preferable to complete the shaping and finishing of the new piece before fitting, in order not to scratch the stock immediately adjoining the repair. Minor adjustments can be made, if necessary, after the repair has been carried out.

Sometimes the fore-end replacement involves making a recess for the barrel loop. In this case, the position of the loop is carefully marked, and using a tiny chisel, about ⅛-inch wide, the recess is carefully cut into it, to exactly the correct depth. If the fore-end has been replaced only on one side, a twist drill of the correct size is inserted into the pin channel on the good side and drilled right through to the new portion, taking care to keep the drill absolutely straight, or the end result will be a pin hole too close to the top or bottom of the stock.

If the entire fore-end has been replaced, the position of the hole in the barrel loop has to be very carefully measured and marked on the stock, and, with the barrel taped in position, using the finest drill available, the pin hole is drilled. If this passes through the hole successfully, the hole can be drilled right through the stock, and the restorer can congratulate himself on a satisfactorily completed job.

The use of a fine drill permits some adjustment in the direction of the channel, should this be necessary, as the hole has to be enlarged to accommodate the barrel pins, and this can be done with a rat-tail file in the direction necessary to ensure a perfect alignment of pin and loop, with the barrel securely fitted at the bottom of the stock recess. Caution should be taken that undue pressure is not exerted laterally on the twist drill,

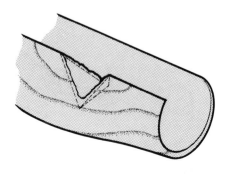
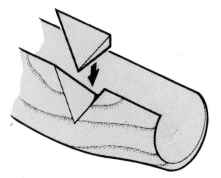

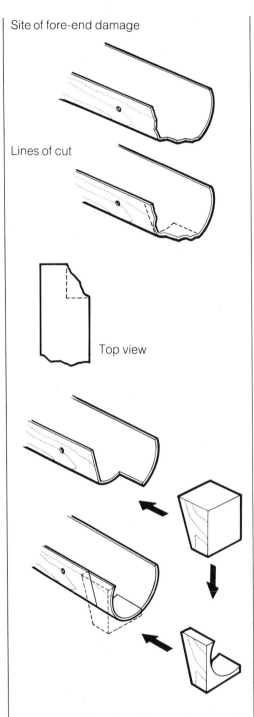

Site of fore-end damage

Lines of cut

Top view

accommodate the wedge.

Although stock repairs are almost always best carried out by splicing techniques, there are some areas in which wood filler should be employed. Small holes in the stock come into this category, especially worm holes. The other important use for this material is in the repair of that part of the stock where the barrel pins are inserted. Sometimes, due to careless insertion of these pins, a tiny chunk of wood is knocked out at this point, and even if this has not occurred, the holes often tend to show a somewhat moth-eaten appearance, which can easily be improved. Although in the former case a piece of wood can be spliced in, this is a difficult repair, and I believe that it is always obvious. This is not the case if wood filler is used.

Make up a small quantity of epoxy resin. Then take a piece of walnut and sand it down, using medium- or fine-grade sandpaper, collecting all the walnut sawdust on a piece of white paper. Add a little of this to the resin and mix it with a penknife. Add a little more, and mix again. Continue to do this until the mixture appears quite dry and looks more like wood than glue. Remove the barrel pin, and clean the hole with carbon tetrachloride. When dry, the filler is applied to the hole. Using the barrel pin, a hole is created in the centre of the filler. This will make subsequent fitting much easier. When dry, the filler is sanded down; whiskering is not necessary and no joins will be seen, provided the edges are carefully sanded. A rat-tail file can be used to smooth off and enlarge the hole, to allow the pin to be inserted. When subsequently inserting the pin, always take care not to knock out the filler. The pin should therefore, in the future, always be inserted from this side.

Dents in the stock can be removed by soaking a cloth or a few layers of tissue in water, placing it over the dent and pressing it with the point of a hot iron. This raises the grain, and can be repeated several times until the dent disappears completely. Afterwards the stock may require very light sanding and whiskering, before staining.

When sanding a gunstock it is absolutely essential to sand *in the direction* of the grain.

Splits in the stock, such as those which sometimes occur in the stock below the lock, are dealt with in the following way.

First, take a piece of thick paper and slip it inside the split as far as the apex. Then push it to and fro to clean any dirt and dust from its edges. Epoxy resin is then applied, widening the crack with the fingers to ensure complete coverage by

as this will very easily break, leaving the restorer in a very unenviable predicament. Only the hand drill should be used for this job.

When barrel wedges are used, several drill holes are made and filed into each other. The use of a flat Swiss file will then enlarge the hole to

158

the adhesive, and the split is then compressed by means of a clamp – always protecting the stock by means of wood blocks. The excess adhesive is wiped away and the repair left for forty-eight hours. This method will effectively repair any crack, and any remaining traces of adhesive can be removed with the thumb nail or wire wool.

A situation which the restorer will undoubtedly encounter occurs when a woodscrew securing the lock, or perhaps the barrel tang or butt-cap, continues to turn endlessly without gripping the wood, having worn the female thread in the stock. To repair this is simple yet very effective. The width of the entry hole should be checked and its depth measured. Using a drill of the next largest size, a hole is drilled in the stock, slightly larger than the existing one. A piece of wood dowelling of suitable width is obtained, sanded down to fit if necessary, and cut to the correct length. It is then rounded off at the bottom to correspond with the contour of the drilled hole and flattened slightly along its length. Glue is applied to the bottom and side and it is pressed into place, the flattened edge permitting air and excess adhesive to escape and allowing the dowel to slip easily to the bottom of the pre-drilled hole. After drying for twenty-four hours, a hole is drilled down the centre to the depth of the screw and the width of the core of the screw. Taking a drill of the same width as the shank of the screw, the upper part of the hole is enlarged. The screw is then applied to the hole and screwed in slowly and carefully. It should cut its own thread but, if the accommodating hole is not large enough, driving the screw in could split the stock.

If there is any resistance, the depth of the hole and the length and width of its components should be checked, and adjusted if necessary. When completed, the stock should be turned over and any wood debris tapped out, after which light staining of the tell-tale white wood hole will render this repair undetectable.

STOCK FINISHING

Very often an old gun will be acquired which has been varnished, and especially if new wood has to be inserted it is advisable first to strip off all the old varnish. This is best done with liquid paint stripper and wire wool. For the first time the new owner will be able to see the natural beauty of the walnut grain. Some parts of the stock may require to be sanded to remove dents or scores in the wood and the 'iron' technique may have to be employed. In any event, all these procedures tend to open the grain of the wood and, therefore, before the stock can be polished, walnut grain filler, obtainable from D-I-Y shops, is applied across the grain. This filler can also disguise deep scores and shallow holes in the stock. After leaving for twenty-four hours, the excess grain filler is sanded off. It will not always be necessary to perform this task, and the restorer learns to 'see' when the grain is open and, therefore, when this technique must be employed.

If the stock has lost its colour, at this stage apply one coat of raw linseed oil and leave for another twenty-four hours.

Then, making a 'rubber' of cotton wool surrounded by any hairless material, one or two coats of button polish are applied to the entire stock. This is not intended as a finish, but merely to seal the grain before polishing. After leaving for twenty-four hours, the button polish is dulled down, using 000 steel wool. The stock is polished, either by applying several coats of wax polish until the desired finish is obtained or by using the linseed-oil technique. This is the method which I prefer, although much more laborious, and consists of hand-rubbing the stock with a small amount of boiled linseed oil twice daily for up to a month. After this time, the application of hard wax completes the polishing process, and it only requires a little of this polish applied once or twice a year to keep the gunstock in perfect condition.

SCREWS

The main difficulty with screws which the restorer is likely to come across is, not unnaturally, in their extraction. Many antique firearms have lain neglected for over two centuries, and the metal parts have become rusted. Previous attempts to remove stubborn screws usually result in screw slots that have become worn at either end.

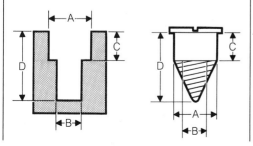

Cased silver-mounted percussion pistols. Note original blueing on the barrels

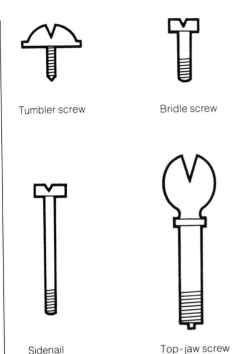

Tumbler screw

Bridle screw

Sidenail

Top-jaw screw

No attempt to remove stubborn screws should be made without using a well-fitting screwdriver, which penetrates to the bottom of the slot. A slow and even pressure should be exerted. Sometimes, if clockwise pressure is exerted first, followed by the normal anti-clockwise movement, a screw will start to come out. Sharply tapping the screwdriver with a hammer may have the same effect. Metal screws should always be treated first with release oil, applied if necessary over a period of days.

Sometimes the screw is so worn that there is no possible hope of extraction without deepening the screw slot. This can be done by repeated scoring with a scriber or the sharp blade of a narrow screwdriver. Such a procedure is very laborious, but well worth employing. Sometimes a sharp knife file will produce the same effect. If there is no original finish on the weapon, the best method of removing screws that are well and truly stuck is the application of heat. This must never be done where there are even slight traces of blueing or browning on the weapon, or these will be lost for ever. The heat is applied by means of a blow torch, and if heated bright red will burn off any old oil or grease, while the expansion and contraction of the metal will loosen rust. When cool, the screw will easily turn.

Only on one occasion was I driven to the very last resort, the ultimate expression of total failure, which I am always loathe to execute – drilling the screw out. This is done by centre-popping the screw head and drilling through it, using a drill of approximately half the diameter of the screw head. If unsuccessful, the next largest size drill is used, when the head breaks off neatly at the shank and the part it secures can be removed. The hand vice applied to the shank will normally unscrew the offending item in the usual way. Occasionally it may be necessary to drill as far as the female thread. Great care must be taken to avoid damage to this thread. Successively larger drills can be used, and the last rim of the screw can be removed with the sharpened point of an $\frac{1}{8}$-inch metal rod. Such a tool can be very useful in the workshop, and can be mounted for convenience in a short wooden handle.

Once a difficult screw has been removed, it can usually be repaired. The screw is inserted in the vice, using the protective jaws. The distorted slot can often be repaired to a greater or lesser degree by tapping either side of the slot with a large pin punch and a 4 oz hammer. The slot is deepened with a Junior hacksaw blade or, in the case of a smaller screw, with a knife file. Afterwards the head should be cleaned up, using emery cloth and fine wet and dry sandpaper, before polishing with wire wool.

The thread normally employed in English guns is of the B.A. type. One cannot, however, buy this type of screw, since they normally have a smooth shank. Thus, these screws have to be specially made. Access to an engineering shop, or having a friend who can use a lathe, is therefore essential to the restorer. Failing these, an antique gunsmith will do the job with ease. It is, however, preferable to have one's own lathe, and although I myself was never very proficient in its use, it is amazing what can be achieved with a sharp tool and a good set of files! Top-jaw screws, in particular, became a speciality. In cutting screw slots, it should be noted that after using the Junior hacksaw blade, the slots of all screws other than lock screws should be tapered with a knife file.

Sometimes it is necessary to replace the wood screws securing the stock to the top or back strap. These screws were generally contoured to the shape of the strap, but if a modern screw of the correct length and size of screwhead is inserted, it will be found to stand well up above the strap and it requires very patient work with the file on the countersunk portion of the screw to allow it to seat into position on the strap. The screw head will still be found to stand proud of the surface of the strap, and must now be filed to fit. This is done by marking the screw with a scribe at the point where filing is required. The screw is then removed, filing is carried out from one end of the head to the other, and the screw replaced. After repeatedly working in this way, the desired contour is obtained. The screw is finally removed, the slot deepened and the surface sanded and polished. The screw is then aged as necessary, before replacing in position.

NIPPLES

Sometimes the nipples of old percussion weapons will be found to be damaged, very often by children, but sometimes by adults, who will cock the hammer of an old gun and press the trigger, allowing the hammer to fall on the unprotected nipple. This practice will eventually wear the nipple down, break it off entirely or, even worse, fracture the hammer itself, whose metal may have crystallized with age. The antique firearms collector will never abuse his collection in this way, and will invariably warn those who handle his weapons against this type of treatment.

In order to remove percussion nipples, release oil must be applied for several days, preferably by jamming a tiny piece of hardwood dowelling down the hole in its centre, inverting the weapon, and pouring release oil down the barrel.

If the squared portion of the nipple is intact, a nipple key of the correct size is placed over it and the nipple extracted. Should there be a complete absence of barrel finish, heat applied by means of a blowlamp will assist in its removal, but before embarking on this procedure please ensure that the weapon is not loaded – a not uncommon occurrence!

If all else fails, the nipple must be drilled out. This is done using successively larger drills, taking extreme care not to damage the female thread. When only a thin shell remains of the nipple, this can be removed using the sharpened steel point already described.

Turning a new nipple in the lathe is a fairly straightforward exercise. If, however, no lathe is available, a nipple can be purchased from an antique gunsmith. It is essential to indicate the height of the nipple required, and the thread size, but it is probably easier to bring the barrel along and fit your own. I usually have a stock of B.A. screws around so that I can immediately tell the size of a particular screw hole and, indeed, I also have a complete set of female threads so that screws can be 'sized up' in a similar way.

It is pointless to fit a nipple which is absolutely pristine, and with all its edges crisp and sharp, to a gun which exhibits signs of wear, so any sharp edges should be very slightly radiused with a smooth file and the nipple matched in colour to the rest of the barrel.

BARREL PINS AND WEDGES

Barrel pins may be missing from antique weapons and, in some instances, may not extend across the full width of the stock.

Pins are easily constructed in the lathe by filing down 2-inch nails, but may otherwise be fabricated by clamping the nail in the vice and filing and sanding it to the required thickness, using emery cloth applied in a see-saw motion. With care, a nicely rounded pin can be constructed.

A dome head is filed in on one side, and it is then pushed into its guide hole. The dome should be just proud of the surface of the stock. The desired length is marked on the opposite side with a scribe or knife file, and the pin removed, cut across and domed as on the opposite side. Sometimes the barrel pin may become loose in its socket and, if this is the case, it is placed in the vice, and tapped lightly with the 4 oz hammer to produce a slight bend at its centre. When replaced, it will be found to be a tight fit once again.

Flat barrel pins, or wedges, are constructed by filing from a block of mild steel. This should be slightly longer than required, to allow for fitting. It is then reduced in width and thickness, leaving the

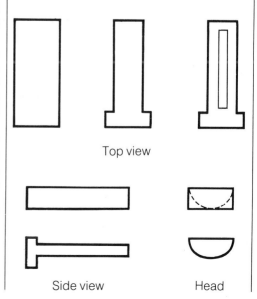

Top view

Side view   Head

163

head for shaping at a later stage. The slot is made by drilling several holes along a central line, and filing them into one another. Adjustment of thickness is carried out as necessary, the head is shaped, and the length shortened to fit the stock.

RAMRODS

These are best constructed from a length of square-section walnut. A rod is inserted into the ramrod groove to ascertain the exact length required. This is then marked off on the walnut, which is fixed in the vice and reduced to approximately rounded section, using a spokeshave or wood rasp. As it begins to approach the required shape, it is sanded down with rough sandpaper, repeatedly turning over in the hand to maintain symmetry. An attempt should now be made to fit it into the ramrod pipes, in order to give some idea of how much more remains to be sanded. The process continues until the new ramrod begins to slide through the second ramrod pipe. Using medium sandpaper now, the ramrod is sanded once more, and again pushed through the pipes. It will still bind, and should be turned a few times and withdrawn. The point at which binding occurs will show as a shiny round ring. Using fine sandpaper, and concentrating on the shiny area, the ramrod is again sanded, and again fitted and turned.

Proceed gradually in this manner until the ramrod is within one inch of bottoming. At this stage it is probably best to fit the ramrod tip, so that it will still be possible to sand the wood to exactly the same diameter as the base of the tip. This is fitted quite simply by running a sharp penknife blade round the ramrod, half an inch or so from the tip, and reducing the diameter of the terminal portion to the diameter of the hole in the tip, preferably using a medium safety-edge file, to prevent damage to the proximal portion of the ramrod. The ramrod is flattened slightly at this point, and glue is applied before fixing the tip in position. When dry, further sanding is carried out in such a way that the new tip and ramrod are in perfect alignment, and at the same time the ramrod itself is a tight fit in both pipes.

A worm should now be fitted to the lower end. Before 1800, such worms took the form of an uncapped corkscrew, used for removing wads from the bore. After this date, a brass cap incorporating a screw for removing the ball was used.

Measure the length of the worm, and mark off

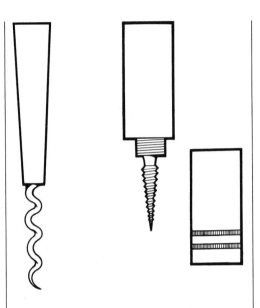

the ramrod accordingly. Ensure that the diameter of the ramrod at this point is at least the diameter of the base of the worm, using a micrometer guage. Run a sharp penknife blade round the ramrod at the point marked, and cut it off half an inch beyond this point. Reduce the diameter of the last half inch of the ramrod, tapering if necessary. Insert the ramrod into the worm, after first glueing the tip. Leave to dry. When dry, smooth off ramrod to the diameter of the base of the worm. The ramrod is then whiskered, before staining and polishing.

Of course, the lathe is the ideal way of making a ramrod, and is also useful for making worms and tips.

Ramrods for fowling pieces are best made from wood dowelling, purchased from D-I-Y shops.

Swivel, or captive, ramrods, which are attached to the barrel by means of a collar and side links, are, I believe, beyond the capacity of the average amateur restorer to construct, and are best ordered from the antique gunsmith or supplier of antique gun parts.

WORMS AND TIPS

These, too, are readily available from antique gunsmiths, and are very easy to fit. Always ensure, however, that the particular one fitted is the correct one for the pistol you are restoring.

Thus, if a pistol has a brass barrel and furniture it is unlikely to have had an ivory-tipped ramrod, and one dating from around 1840 should not have the early form of worm.

TRIGGER-GUARDS

The most common problem encountered with trigger-guards is pitting, resulting from deep-seated rusting and corrosion. Where it affects the interior of the guard, this can be removed without much difficulty, first using a rounded file and then medium through to fine emery cloth, wrapped around the file and rubbed in a to-and-fro motion. It will be found easier to sand across the guard, but once the pitting has been removed the sanding must be carried out in the direction of the 'grain', because grain exists even in metal. First using medium emery cloth, followed by fine, and then applying the finer grades of wet and dry sandpaper, the metal is brought to a high polish. It will seen, however, that the scratches from the filing and sanding will still be in evidence across the grain, and these must be removed by further rubbing in a longitudinal direction. The resulting smoothly polished metal is infinitely preferable to the deep scars of old pitting.

Unfortunately, the exterior of the trigger-guard presents a more difficult problem since almost certainly there will be borderline engraving, and possibly a rose or other motif at its centre.

Sandpapering with emery cloth will undoubtedly remove this for ever, so it is essential, if the weapon is to be properly restored, that one has access to a good engraver. Restorers usually have such engravers tucked away somewhere, and guard them zealously against any incomers.

Good engravers, capable of carrying out the high-quality work of their 18th-century forebears, are hard to come by, and their services are very expensive. Most are reluctant to work on steel, especially hardened steel, and if possible the part should be heated to bright red heat, in order to anneal the metal.

Instructions to the engraver should be very explicit, in order to avoid later disappointment. Every detail should be covered – the size and style of any lettering, the length of the signature, the depth of the engraving, and so on. I personally see no reason why old engraving, if faint, should not be recut, or 'sharpened', although some purists would stop short of this.

Provided one has obtained the services of such an engraver, the restoration of the exterior of the guard can proceed in exactly the same way as the interior, and the metal aged as described later in this chapter. All new engraving should be lightly rubbed with wet and dry sandpaper, in order to remove the tell-tale burr.

BUTT-CAPS AND SIDEPLATES

Silver grotesque masks and sideplates for Queen Anne pistols are available for purchase from firms specializing in antique gun parts. Certain specific patterns are also available, e.g. sideplates for 12-inch Dragoon pistols, Sea-service pistols, etc.

COCKS AND HAMMERS

A certain amount of repair work is possible with these items. A common finding is the absence of the top-jaw and screw, and these can be ordered in the normal way from the specialist suppliers. It is safer to send the cock itself, in order to obtain the correct pattern. It is not difficult to make a top-jaw from a piece of mild steel. In order to facilitate this procedure, however, it is well worth making a very useful tool, which can be employed in many aspects of gun repair work. This is a block of mild steel, about $2\frac{1}{2}$ inches in length and $\frac{1}{2}$-inch square. A hole is drilled at the top, and tapped to 2 B.A. thread size. An Allen cap-head screw of this size should be purchased. With this little gadget, and a few washers, many gun parts can be very firmly secured in the vice while cutting, filing or polishing metal parts.

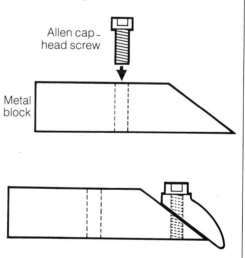

Top-jaw fixed in position for shaping

If the end is ground off at an angle and another hole drilled on the slope, this makes many jobs much easier. In making a top-jaws, one of 2 B.A. size and another of 0 B.A. size will be invaluable.

The method of making a top-jaw is to first drill the hole for the retaining screw before placing on top of the lower jaw, scribing the outline and filing to shape.

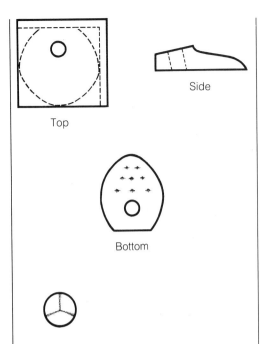

Top

Side

Bottom

A wider piece than necessary is used to allow for adjustment after drilling.

Tooth marks are created in the bottom by means of a punch ground to a triangular point, as shown in the diagram. This aids in gripping the leather covering the flint.

The comb of the cock may be broken, or the hammer spur broken off. It is not difficult to have a small piece of steel welded on and the cock or hammer shaped in the correct proportions. In the case of a hammer, the new spur will require to be chequered by the engraver.

Most garages have welding equipment and are capable of carrying out welding repairs of a very high standard. After welding the part will require to be cleaned using fine-grade wet and dry sandpaper and wire wool, and engraving can be carried out as necessary.

On no account should electric arc welding be employed in the repair of antique gun parts. Oxyacetylene should invariably be used.

Replacement hammers and cocks can be ordered from the suppliers, whose catalogues cover a wide variety of pistols and long guns, and there should be no difficulty in obtaining replacements.

The 'throw', that is, the distance from the centre of the tumbler screw to the nipple, in the case of a percussion hammer, or from that point to the toe of the top-jaw, must be specified.

I have frequently been able to use such castings without any refinishing, other than careful ageing, but sometimes they do require a little filing and sanding before use. The cock may have to be tapped out to receive the top-jaw screw, and the top-jaw itself may require drilling.

When the hammer casting arrives, it will not be drilled and squared off for the tumbler. The method of doing this consists of centrepopping the hammer and drilling a small hole. A round paper sticker, of the type used in marking photographic slides, is stuck over the inside face, with the drilled hole at its centre. The hammer is held over the tumbler in what would be its normal position when resting on the nipple, but is rotated forwards a few degrees, beyond the nipple. It is held in this position and tapped with a hammer. This causes the outline of the tumbler to be impressed on the paper sticker.

The reason for this elaborate procedure is to ensure that the pressure of the mainspring will hold the hammer tightly against the nipple, even in the uncocked state, and therefore it is very important that the exact position of the tumbler square is determined.

Now use a centre punch to mark the position of each corner of the tumbler square. Finally, remove the paper marker and use a scriber to join the centrepops and show the outline of the tumbler square.

All that is required now is to enlarge the central hole and complete the square, using a square tapering file. After some fine adjustments, the hammer can be fitted over the tumbler square.

The hammer nose will probably require to be drilled. This should be carried out after centre-popping, and using successively larger drills until only a thin rim remains. The internal surface should then be blackened as described later in this chapter.

A loose hammer or cock is anathema to the collector, and can be tightened up by placing the cock on an anvil, preferably working on the inside face, since dents will be created in the metal which may not be entirely hidden by the tumbler screw and, using an 8 oz hammer and heavy pin punch, hammering around the margins of the square. By trial and error, any hammer may be tightened up in this way.

RAMROD PIPES

These, too, are available from suppliers. For lathe owners they represent a simple turning job. Place the completed pipe in the ramrod groove and scribe the position of the tab on the top surface. A brass tab of the correct size is then silver soldered into position. The pipe is replaced in the groove, and the position of its securing pin marked by inserting a tiny drill through the pin channel. The pipe is removed once more, and the pin hole drilled through it. It is finally secured in position by means of a large-diameter panel pin cut to the correct size.

Silver soldering is a technique which can be readily mastered even by the amateur restorer, and will permit him to carry out a far broader spectrum of repairs. It is important to ensure that the parts to be joined are scrupulously clean. They are then placed on a small firebrick in close apposition. Another firebrick should be placed at the rear to concentrate the heat. The parts are then heated in the blowlamp to a temperature approaching red heat. Flux is applied at this stage, and bubbles away for a little while before forming a liquid. At this point, silver solder is run into the joint.

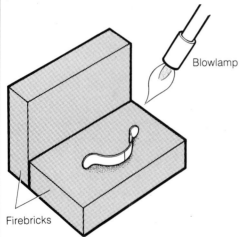

Blowlamp

Firebricks

Sometimes it is helpful to direct the silver solder into the joint using a metal rod. If the joint will have to take any stress as, for example, in silver soldering a broken hammer, where the broken part has not been lost, a tiny hole should be drilled in each part and a panel pin inserted. This not only increases the strength of the joint, but brings the parts into closer apposition.

If the material is very thin, as it might be in the case of a trigger-guard, it is helpful to increase the amount of solder in the joint by chamfering both edges of one side of the joint and running the silver solder round.

The excess of flux should be removed by immersion in boiling water, while any excess of

silver solder can be easily removed with a fine file, and the part can be polished in the usual way.

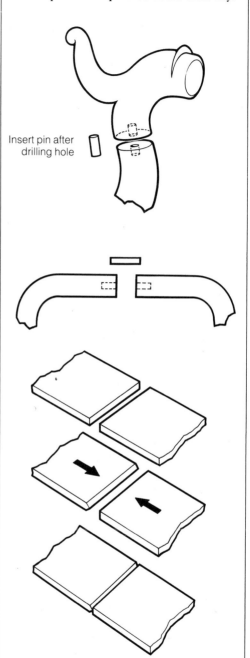

Insert pin after drilling hole

Chamfer edges when joining thin metal

Cased Pocket Colt revolver

BARRELS

Before starting to work on any gun barrel, it should be examined to make sure that it is not loaded. Obstructions in the bore can be removed using a ramrod with attached worm.

The double corkscrew type will remove wadding or other soft material. If the weapon is loaded, the ball can be extracted by means of a screw jag, which can be screwed into the soft lead.

Light superficial rusting can conveniently be removed by gentle rubbing with wire wool soaked in oil. This will preserve any browning remaining on the barrel, but should nevertheless be done with great care. If there is much superficial rust, the barrel can be soaked in oil for several days to soften this. Small patches can be removed by applying oil and laying a fine round file across it. When the file is moved gently to and fro under its own weight, the loosened particles of rust float up onto the surface of the oil. No pressure should be exerted or the finish will be disturbed.

If there is any pitting on the barrel, a decision must be made as to whether this should be removed. Slight pitting on a barrel retaining its original finish must be ignored, since removing the pits will inevitably destroy the finish as well. A note should be made of any signature or other engraving and, if at all possible, this part of the barrel should be avoided. The upper limit of the stock should be marked with a pencil down either side of the barrel, and no filing or sanding should be allowed to proceed beyond this point, since to do so would make the barrel a loose fit in the stock.

The barrel is then placed in the vice, protected by wooden blocks cut to shape. The pitting is filed off, preferably using long, even strokes, in a longitudinal direction. Emery cloth of medium grade is next used, employed in a see-saw fashion to maintain symmetry. When all file marks have been removed, the cloth must be employed in a longitudinal direction and, working through wet and dry sandpaper to fine wire wool of 000 grade, the barrel is then brought to a polish. Care must be taken not to encroach on the pencil line.

Octagonal barrels require very careful work to maintain the symmetry of their shape. Again use long, even strokes, applied in a longitudinal direction, finishing off with fine emery cloth wrapped around a file or flat piece of wood. The job is completed using fine wet and dry sandpaper and wire wool.

The bore of the weapon may be cleaned of rust with a proprietary derusting solution. However, my own preference, provided the rusting is minimal, is to pour release oil down the barrel in order to soften it, before rubbing vigorously with a modern phosphorbronze brush on the end of a cleaning rod. Minor pitting can be removed by means of a piece of wood dowelling to which emery cloth has been pinned, but deep pitting may necessitate the use of a round file in the first instance. Following the removal of rust, the bore may be burnished with wire wool wrapped around the brush. The barrel interior is then mopped out, and a few drops of oil instilled to prevent futher rusting.

When cleaning it is preferable to unscrew any screwbarrel pistols. Many, however, are unfortunately seized up by the accumulation of dirt and rust in the threads. There are two methods of unscrewing such barrels. The first consists of blocking up the vent or nipple with a tiny piece of hardwood dowel and pouring enough release oil down the barrel to cover the internal screw thread. It may take several weeks for the oil to penetrate, and as this tends to seep away through the vent or nipple, it should be 'topped up' as necessary. With the pistol firmly held between blocks in the vice, insulation tape is wound very thickly round the barrel to avoid damage from the jaws of the wrench we intend to employ. This is then fitted around the tape, and the barrel will then, hopefully, unscrew.

If this method is unsuccessful, and there is no original finish whatsoever on the pistol, the barrel is then heated at the screw-off point until it becomes red hot. This burns off all the old oil and dirt and, when cool, the tape is again wrapped around the barrel, which should then unscrew. It is essential to ensure that the jaws of the wrench do not penetrate the tape, and I usually reinforce the tape with a strip of phosphorbronze.

LOCKPLATES

Lockplates may be treated in a similar manner to barrels. However, as there is almost invariably engraving on the lockplate, it must be considered whether this should be sacrificed in order to remove pitting. It may be that the surface is only rusted, without actual pitting and, if this is the case, the rust can be removed by rubbing with progressively finer grades of wet and dry sandpaper and wire wool, without damaging the engraving.

Lock parts, if absent, can be ordered, but a good deal of work would be necessary to fit these to any given lock, and it is probably better either to send the lockplate to the supplier or to approach your old friend, the antique gunsmith.

Locks that are badly rusted can be treated by simmering in caustic-soda solution. Doing this indoors is a course of action likely to end in the divorce courts, and I would recommend that this be carried out using a camping gas stove, and out of doors, since the fumes are extremely pungent, and the solution is constantly boiling over. Afterwards the parts will require to be burnished.

A faulty action is frequently caused by wear occurring at the half- and full-cock bents, usually the former, which is cut back slightly, so that when the sear is engaged it is unable to slip out. Using fine files, the bents can be straightened, and a knife file will restore the recess for the sear nose. If this, too, is worn, it can be very quickly reshaped.

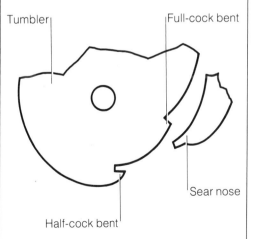

Tumbler
Full-cock bent
Half-cock bent
Sear nose

FRIZZENS

These may be found to be very pitted indeed. Removal of this pitting is often extremely difficult, since frizzens are invariably hardened. Heating bright red in the blowlamp flame may soften the frizzen sufficiently for the file to be used, before final sandpapering. If much surface metal has been removed, it is a good plan to re-create the scored appearance caused by repeated contact with flints over a period of many years. These marks can be filed in, or reproduced by means of coarse emery cloth, after first measuring the upper limit of contact with the flint. Any burr should be removed by light sanding with wet and dry sandpaper.

Replacement frizzens can, if necessary, be purchased from the specialist suppliers.

SPRINGS

Making springs is a very arduous and highly skilled task, which I believe is best left to the specialist gunsmith. It is, however, within the capabilities of the amateur restorer to make certain types of spring, including pawl springs for revolvers and pepperboxes, powder flask cut-off springs and revolver trigger springs. Revolver mainsprings of Colt type, which do not require a great deal of filing and shaping, may also be attempted.

However, the normal V-type flintlock or percussion-lock mainspring requires very careful measurement and laborious filing, and is the most difficult type of spring to construct.

Lengths of spring steel of various thicknesses are available for purchase. One of suitable thickness is selected, cut to size and filed to the correct shape. It is then polished before heating to a bright cherry red. It is now possible to bend the spring to the required shape, and a hole can be drilled for the retaining screw. The spring is again heated to cherry red, and cooled by immersion in cold water.

It is then polished a second time, and suspended from a light wire. Heat is again applied, when the metal will begin to change colour, becoming first straw-coloured, and soon changing to blue. As soon as the straw colour appears, the spring should be quenched in oil.

This completes the tempering process, and the spring should now be able to take the stresses required of it.

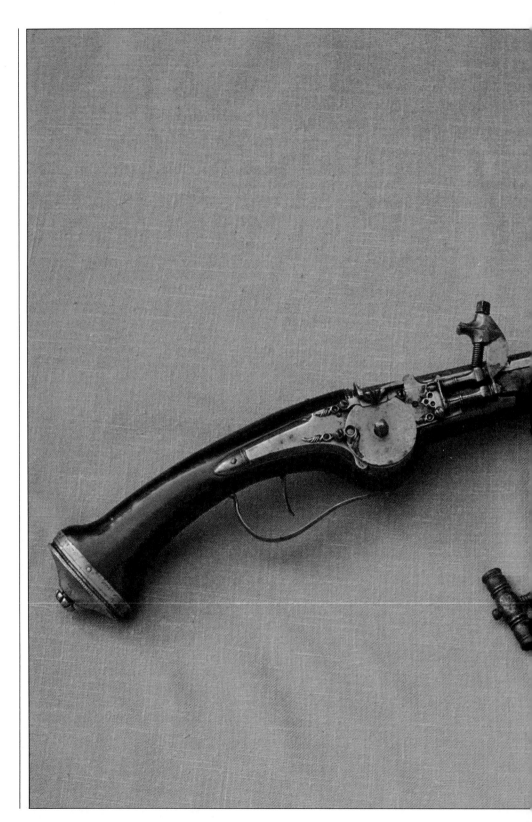

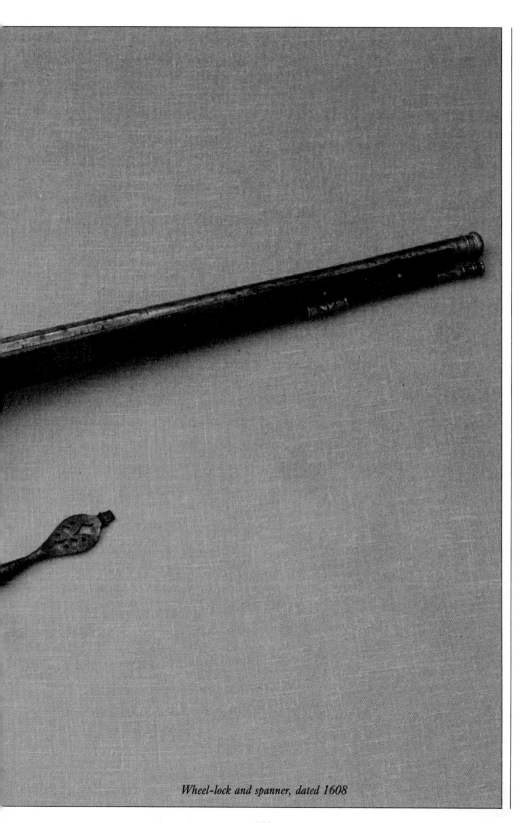

Wheel-lock and spanner, dated 1608

BLUEING AND BROWNING

Blueing

It is, in my opinion, virtually impossible for any amateur to endeavour to match the unmistakable shade of blue attained by the gunsmiths of the 18th century, and no attempt should be made to colour barrels which retain some of this original finish. However, many percussion guns have a form of blueing known as charcoal blueing, and this, on the other hand, is very simple to patch up, if it is partially deficient. The barrel is first degreased by pouring boiling water over it. Any droplets remaining quickly evaporate, but the method works best if the barrel is still hot. 'Quick blue' solution, obtained from a gunsmith, is used. A piece of cottonwool is dipped into the solution, which is then applied to the deficient patches. After drying, all traces should be washed off with boiling water. The part refinished will have a dark blue or black colour, which can be deepened if required by further application of the solution. All metal parts may be treated in this way if desired.

Browning

A wooden plug is first inserted down the barrel, as during the process of browning the barrel must not be touched by hand. The barrel is then degreased, either by using boiling water or by application of carbon tetrachloride. Browning solution is then wiped on with cottonwool, applied in longitudinal strokes. Runs should be avoided, since these will show up later, as the rust begins to form. Another method consists of light dabbing of the barrel, as this prevents the formation of runs.

The barrel is put on one side for twelve hours. After this time, it will be found to be covered in light rust. This is rubbed off with fine wire wool, and the solution applied again. Every twelve hours the process is repeated, until eventually a brown coloration begins to show up in the metal, which does not disappear when sanded off with wire wool.

Continue for a total of twenty-eight coats, when the maximum depth of colour is achieved. The barrel should then be thoroughly washed off with boiling water and, when still hot, boiled linseed oil should be rubbed in with an old rag. Once dry, the barrel can be polished with a soft cloth, and the end result will be a barrel magnificently browned to the standards of the gunmakers of old. Browning should never be applied to barrels which are pitted.

The solution which I employ is:

Corrosive sublimate	7g
Spirit of Wine	28ml
Tincture of Ferric Perchloride	28ml
Distilled Water	1 litre

A 'Quick brown' solution is also available and may be useful for touching up.

AGEING

I have already mentioned the futility of fitting bright new parts to old guns, and it is thus important that these parts are 'aged', in order to blend in with the old.

Equally, barrels from which the pitting has been removed are now highly polished, and this obviously looks quite incongruous considering the age of the piece.

Before considering the methods involved in artificially reproducing the effects of age, it is imperative that the restorer adopts the critical eye of the artist. Up until now he has been solely concerned with the removal of the familiar black discoloration of old rust, but now this process is reversed, as an attempt is made to re-create this darkened appearance. However, as the surface metal has now been fully restored, further darkening becomes completely acceptable.

There are two methods of darkening metal parts. The first consists of degreasing the parts, and in the application of 'quick blue' solution. This causes consequent darkening of the parts, which can then be lightened to the desired shade, either by rubbing with a piece of cloth or by dabbing with fine wire wool soaked in oil. The solution must be neutralized after use by pouring boiling water over the part. This method is very rapid, and is excellent for filling in new engraving. However, the colour imparted can be detected by the experienced eye, having a characteristic dull sheen.

If not satisfied with the colour produced, the process can be repeated until the desired shade is achieved.

My own preference, in ageing metal, lies in the use of browning fluid. The process is exactly the same as in browning itself, but the solution is always dabbed on, this producing a more uniform result. After twenty-four hours, the part should be inspected to ensure that the rusting solution has been taken up uniformly, without patches. If not, the part must be sanded off, degreased, and the solution reapplied very carefully. Forceps should be used to handle the parts.

After twenty-four to forty-eight hours, the metal surface should be quite rusted. As it is vital that this does not proceed to actual pitting, it is important to observe the rusting process at regular intervals. The part should then be immersed in boiling water and boiled for several minutes. It is then removed and allowed to rust for a few days. It is then boiled again, after which it will be found to have gone completely black. The extent to which this blackening is removed is determined by the depth of colour the restorer wishes to achieve. Even if completely removed by wire wool soaked in oil, the metal parts will no longer be the colour they exhibited before treatment. They are of a much duller hue, and this type of finish is ideal for the military pistol.

On the other hand, if not rubbed off but lightly dabbed, the resultant finish is slightly more aged in appearance, with spots here and there similar to tiny pinpoints of old rust. The engraving, incidentally, is always blackened, and this, of course, is essential in trying to mimic the effects of age.

Similarly, there is no point in leaving the slots of screws looking bright and shiny, and these can be aged with either solution, the 'quick blue' being the most rapid method.

The restorer must use all his ingenuity and artistic sensibilities. Look at the trigger-guard of a pistol, for example. One would not expect, in a weapon perhaps 200 years old, to find this entirely and uniformly bright. The inner surface of the guard, where dirt would tend to accumulate, would seldom have had the high polish of the exterior, and certainly not after a few years of usage. The restorer should therefore make the inside of the guard just a shade darker than the outside. Those areas of the inside of the guard, near the trigger-plate, where rust might be expected to form, should be made darker still.

Wherever there is a fold or sharp edge in the metal, for example at the bottom of the trigger, an area of blackened metal should be left, by avoiding contact with the wire wool at these points.

Try to imagine where dirt might have accumulated, at what points brasswork would have been difficult to clean, and leave such parts darker. However, the contrast must not be too glaring, and this is where artistic appreciation comes in.

Brass parts are best aged with 'quick blue' solution, and rubbed carefully with wire wool, ensuring that the engraving has been filled and that the contours less accessible to the cleaning duster are lightly darkened.

The inside bend of a swan-neck cock, or the centre of a throat hole cock, are obvious areas for darkening, and one would expect similar darkening around the barrel vent, the interior of the pan and the lockplate inside the frizzen spring.

I consider the ageing of parts to be a most important part of antique firearms restoration, which provides the perfect finishing touch to a job meticulously planned and painstakingly carried out, and the finished product a work of art of which the restorer can be justly proud.

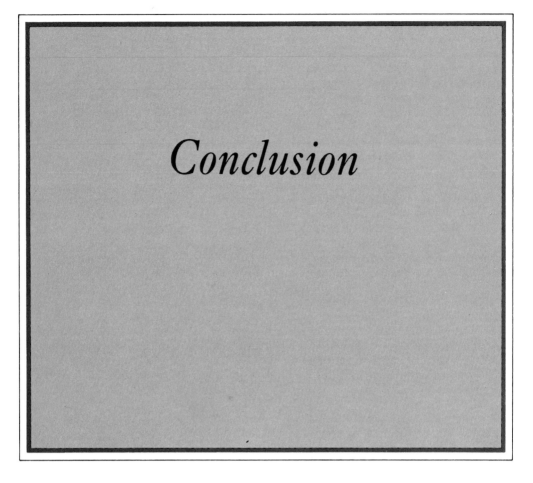

Conclusion

On a fateful afternoon in July 1967, when I tentatively pushed open the door of a tiny antique shop in a small Cheshire town close to my home, I little realized the far-reaching consequences of my action. I have already stated that I stepped across the threshold into a whole new world, and this is the literal truth of the situation.

When I experienced for the first time the thrill of holding in my hands a weapon 200 years old I could scarcely have dreamed of the events which would follow, not merely because this weapon would form the basis of a future collection but also because of the tremendous alteration which has occurred in my life as a result.

It is of inestimable importance that each of us should indulge in some kind of hobby. Life, as we all know, is filled with stresses of many different kinds, and each of us must find some way to unwind, in order to mitigate these stresses to the best of our ability.

The pursuit of antique firearms has been my way of doing just that.

I have attempted to convey the tremendous fascination of this search, since searching is the essence of antique gun collecting. But searching is not the only aspect of collecting.

Study is of equal importance, and embraces not only examination of all the available literature, but of countless specimens of firearms, since it is only through a thorough knowledge of one's subject that one can make any claim to expertise in any particular field.

One can never underestimate the value of the role played by our fellow-collectors, who stimulate and perpetuate our interest, and without whom our own interest would undoubtedly fade, since there can be no greater satisfaction than discussion and critical appraisal of any item with a kindred spirit.

The true collector is an enthusiast, a man whose goal can never be reached, whose collection is never completed, since his latest acquisition is still awaiting him, just around the next corner. . . .

Bibliography

Antique Firearms, F. Wilkinson. 1970. London. Hamlyn.

Antique Firearms – Their Care, Repair, and Restoration, R. Lister. 1963. London. Jenkins.

Antique Pistol Collecting, Frith and Andrews. 1960. London. Holland Press.

The Book of the Gun, H. L. Peterson. 1963. London. Hamlyn.

British Military Firearms, 1650–1850, H. L. Blackmore. 1961. London. H. Jenkins.

British Pistols and Guns 1610–1840, I. Glendenning. 1951. New York. Arco.

Colt Firearms, J. Serven. 1954. Pennsylvania. Stackpole.

Duelling Pistols, J. Atkinson. 1964. London. Cassell.

English, Irish, and Scottish Firearms Makers, A. M. Carey. 1954. London. Unwin.

English Pistols, H. L. Blackmore. 1985. London. Arms and Armour Press.

Georgian Pistols, N. Dixon. 1971. London. Clowes.

Guns, F. Wilkinson. 1970. London. Hamlyn.

Gun Collecting, G. Boothroyd. 1963. London. Arco.

Gun Collecting, F. Wilkinson. 1974. London. Hamlyn.

The Pleasure of Guns, J. Rosa and R. May. 1974. London. Octopus.

Powder Flask Book, R. Riling. 1953. New York. Bonanza Books.

Remington Handguns, Carr. New York. Bonanza Books.

The Revolver, 1818–1865, Taylerson. 1968. London. Jenkins.

Small Arms, F. Wilkinson. 1965. London. Ward Lock and Co.

Weapons of the British Soldier, Col. Rogers. 1960. London. Sphere Books.

The World's Great Guns, F. Wilkinson. 1969. London. Guinness Signatures.

Index